John J. Pinkerton

A Practical Guide to Administrators, Guardians and Assignees

Containing Full and Complete Instructions for the Settlement of Estates

John J. Pinkerton

A Practical Guide to Administrators, Guardians and Assignees
Containing Full and Complete Instructions for the Settlement of Estates

ISBN/EAN: 9783337402051

Printed in Europe, USA, Canada, Australia, Japan

Cover: Foto ©Suzi / pixelio.de

More available books at **www.hansebooks.com**

A PRACTICAL GUIDE

TO

ADMINISTRATORS, GUARDIANS,

AND

ASSIGNEES,

CONTAINING

FULL AND COMPLETE INSTRUCTIONS FOR THE SETTLEMENT OF ESTATES; TOGETHER WITH ALL THE NECESSARY FORMS, EXPLANATIONS, AND DIRECTIONS.

BY

JOHN J. PINKERTON,
COUNSELLOR AT LAW.

PHILADELPHIA:
KAY & BROTHER,
LAW BOOKSELLERS, PUBLISHERS, AND IMPORTERS.
17 AND 19 SOUTH SIXTH STREET.
1870.

PREFACE.

This little book, it is proper to say, is not intended to assist in making "every man his own lawyer:" those venturing upon that experiment, seldom failing to illustrate the truth of the proverb about "having a fool for a client."

In the collection and preparation of the matter, the sole object in view has been, to put into cheap and convenient form, such a hand book for Administrators, Guardians and Assignees, as would aid them in the performance of their duties. To make it, as far as possible, a thoroughly accurate and reliable authority upon the subjects of which it treats; and to embody all the information requisite in the settlement of any ordinary estate.

A plain style, as devoid of technical terms as possible, has been attempted, that the work may be the more acceptable to non-professional readers. To avoid confusion, names and dates, have, in every instance, been supplied, instead of leaving blank spaces to be afterwards filled.

Knowing how much the usefulness of any book is increased by the thorough character of its index, I have taken pains to furnish one as full and complete as it was possible to make it.

It gives me great pleasure to acknowledge the obligations I am under, to the valuable work of P. Frazer Smith, Esq., on Procedure.

To Mr. Wayne MacVeagh, Mr. J. Smith Futhey and Mr. George F. Smith, of the West Chester Bar, I am also indebted for their friendly interest in the book, as well as for numerous suggestions and important aid, in its preparation.

It is not pretended that such a manual as this, can help, in any way, to dispense with the assistance of an attorney, but only to supplement it.

To counsel themselves, it may perhaps not be without value, in relieving them from the drudgery of writing papers which require no especial skill in their preparation.

With this hope, the book is submitted to the profession, feeling that for its success, its reliance must be upon their kind indulgence.

JOHN J. PINKERTON.

WEST CHESTER, PA.,
January, 1870.

CONTENTS.

CHAPTER I.
                   Page
THE GRANTING OF ADMINISTRATION,   9

CHAPTER II.
INVENTORY AND APPRAISEMENT,   3

CHAPTER III.
THE WIDOW'S INVENTORY,   16

CHAPTER IV.
SALE OF PERSONAL PROPERTY,   20

CHAPTER V.
SALE OF REAL ESTATE FOR PAYMENT OF DEBTS,   23

CHAPTER VI.
DEED FOR REAL ESTATE OF DECEDENT,   34

CHAPTER VII.

PAYMENT OF DEBTS OF DECEDENT,   38

CHAPTER VIII.

ADMINISTRATION ACCOUNT,   42

CHAPTER IX.

DISTRIBUTION OF THE ESTATE,   45

CHAPTER X.

COLLATERAL INHERITANCE TAX,   49

CHAPTER XI.

INTERNAL REVENUE TAX,   55

CHAPTER XII.

DISCHARGE OF AN ADMINISTRATOR,   58

CHAPTER XIII.

THE APPOINTMENT OF GUARDIAN,   60

CHAPTER XIV.

GUARDIAN'S TRIENNIAL AND FINAL ACCOUNT,   67

CHAPTER XV.

DUTIES OF GUARDIAN,   74

CHAPTER XVI.

ASSIGNMENT FOR THE BENEFIT OF CREDITORS, 79

CHAPTER XVII.

INVENTORY AND APPRAISEMENT, 84

CHAPTER XVIII.

DUTIES OF ASSIGNEES, 93

CHAPTER XIX.

ACCOUNT OF ASSIGNEE, &c., 97

CHAPTER XX.

INTERNAL REVENUE STAMPS, 101

INDEX, 105

A GUIDE TO
ADMINISTRATORS, GUARDIANS, &c.

CHAPTER I.

THE GRANTING OF ADMINISTRATION, &c.

The right to administer upon an estate, is, in Pennsylvania, given first, to the widow or husband, then to the sons, and after them to the daughters. When a stranger is about to administer, a renunciation should be obtained in writing, from those who are by law entitled. The Register of Wills will require such a paper to be filed in his office before granting the letters. It should be signed by *all* having a right to administer.

Renunciation of Right to Administration.

To Hampton Thomas, Esq., Register of Wills of Chester County, Pennsylvania:

Sir.—I, Elizabeth D. Wright, widow of Alexander J. Wright, of Pennsbury township, Chester County, Pennsylvania, deceased, do hereby renounce all my right to letters of administration upon the estate of said deceased, and desire that the same may be granted to Samuel C. Lewis, Esq., of said township. Witness my hand, this twenty-third day of September, A. D., 1868.

ELIZABETH D. WRIGHT.

Before the granting of letters of administration, it is necessary for the administrator to give a bond with two sufficient securities in double the value of the *personal* estate of the decedent.

Form of Bond given by Administrator.

KNOW ALL MEN BY THESE PRESENTS, That we, Samuel C. Lewis, Administrator of Alexander J. Wright, late of Pennsbury township, Chester County, Pennsylvania, deceased, David R. Hayes and John B. Roberts, all of said county, are held and firmly bound unto the Commonwealth of Pennsylvania, in the sum of Twelve thousand one hundred and ninety ($12,190) Dollars, to be paid to the said Commonwealth, to which payment, well and truly to be made, we bind ourselves jointly and severally, for and in the whole, our heirs, executors and administrators, firmly by these presents, Sealed with our Seals, dated the first day of October, in the year of our Lord one thousand eight hundred and sixty-eight.

The conditions of this obligation are such, that if the above bounded Samuel C. Lewis, Administrator of all and singular, the goods, chattels, and credits, of Alexander J. Wright, late of the township of Pennsbury, in said county, deceased, do make or cause to be made, a true and perfect inventory of all and singular the goods, chattels and credits of the said deceased, which have come or shall come to the hands, possession or knowledge of the said Samuel C. Lewis, or into the hands or possession of any other person or persons for him, and the same so made do exhibit or cause to be exhibited into the Register's Office, in the county of Chester, within thirty days of the date hereof, and the same goods, chattels and credits, and all other goods, chattels and credits of the said deceased, at the time of his death, which at any time after, shall come to the hands and possession of the said Samuel C. Lewis, or into the hands or possession of any other person or persons for him, do well and truly administer according to law. And further do make or cause to be made, a true and just account of his said administration, within one year from the date hereof, or when thereunto legally required; and all the rest and residue of the said goods, chattels and credits, which shall be found remaining upon the said administrator's account, the same being first examined and allowed by the Orphans' Court of the county having jurisdiction, shall deliver and pay unto such person or persons as the said Orphans' Court, by their decree or sentence, pursuant to law, shall limit and appoint; and shall well and truly comply with the laws of this Commonwealth relating to collateral inheritances. And if it shall hereafter appear, that any Last Will and Testament was made by the said deceased, and the same shall be proved according to law, if the said Samuel C. Lewis being thereunto required, do surrender the said Letters of Administration into the Register's Office aforesaid, then this obligation to be void, otherwise to remain in full force.

Sealed and delivered in the presence of
William James.
Jacob Reeves.

SAMUEL C. LEWIS. [L. S.]

DAVID R. HAYES. [L. S.]

JOHN B. ROBERTS. [L. S.]

Where the value of the estate, real and personal, does not exceed one thousand dollars, no internal revenue stamp is required. When it exceeds one thousand dollars, a stamp of $1.00 is necessary.

The Administrator must always bear in mind that he has nothing whatever to do with the *real* estate, unless it should become necessary to sell it for the payment of the decedent's debts.

The Administrator has no authority whatever, to rent real estate of the decedent, as the land descends to heirs and not to administrators; and the heirs, as owners, have the right to the rent.[1]

Bond having been given and the letters issuing to him, the Administrator should insert notice in one newspaper published in the county, for six successive weeks.

(1) Haslage *v.* Krugh.   1. Casey, 99.

ADMINISTRATOR.

Form of Notice to Debtors and Creditors.

ESTATE OF ALEXANDER J. WRIGHT, DECEASED:

Letters of Administration on the Estate of Alexander J. Wright, late of Pennsbury township, Chester county, Pennsylvania, deceased have been granted to Samuel C. Lewis, residing in said township, to whom all persons indebted to said estate are requested to make payment, and those having claims or demands, will make known the same without delay.

SAMUEL C. LEWIS,

October 5, 1868. Administrator.

CHAPTER II.

INVENTORY AND APPRAISEMENT.

The Administrator, should, as soon as it is practicable, inform himself as to the amount of the personal estate, collecting all bonds, notes, bills, book accounts and other evidences of debt belonging to the decedent, so that they may be included in the inventory required by law to be made.

Within thirty days from the time *of issuing letters of administration*, an inventory and appraisement must be filed in the Register's office, showing the whole of the *personal* property, debts due the decedent, bonds, notes, &c., &c., so far as the administrator has knowledge of the same. This appraisement should be made by two entirely disinterested persons, they having been previously sworn or affirmed.

Form of Inventory and Appraisement.

STATE OF PENNSYLVANIA, } ss.
CHESTER COUNTY,

Henry Davis and James Long, being duly affirmed, say that they will well and truly, and without prejudice or partiality, value and appraise the goods, chattels, and credits, which were of Alexander J. Wright, late of Pennsbury township, county and State aforesaid, deceased, and in all respects perform their duty as appraisers to the best of their skill and judgment.

Affirmed and subscribed before me, this 20th day of October, 1868.
WM. WHITEHEAD, J. P.

HENRY DAVIS,
JAMES LONG.

Inventory and Appraisement of all the goods, chattels, and credits, of Alexander J. Wright, late of Pennsbury township, Chester County, Pennsylvania, deceased:

One doz. Chairs,	$ 24	00
One Bureau,	30	00
Clock,	12	00
One Looking Glass,	7	00
Bedsteads and Bedding,	39	00
Lot of Straw,	26	00
Plow and Harrow,	17	00
46 bus. Wheat,	69	00
Horse,	130	00
Cow,	75	00
Lot of Fodder,	26	00
15 Sheep,	60	00
Sleigh,	30	00
Harness,	11	00
Lot of Manure,	10	00
Prom. Note of Jas. White,	200	00
50 Shares Bank Stock,	2,500	00
Due Bill of Levi Adams,	106	00
Judg't Bond of Philip Price,	2,530	00
Book Account of Robert Keech,	84	80
Book Account of Joseph Paist,	27	50
Cash,	130	70
	$6,095	00

Taken and Appraised by us, this 20th day of October, A. D., 1868.

HENRY DAVIS,
JAMES LONG.

The Inventory should not include the real estate of the decedent.

The appraisers, are by law, entitled to receive one dollar per day for their services in appraising the estate.

The Administrator should be careful to take a receipt from every one to whom he pays money on account of the settlement of the estate. The better course is to procure a receipt book, and thus avoid the danger of mislaying or losing papers. The receipt should in every instance, specify on what account the money was expended.

Form of Receipt taken by Administrator.

Received, West Chester, Pa., November 30, 1868, of Samuel C. Lewis, administrator of Alexander J. Wright, deceased, Six dollars for advertising notice to creditors, &c., and printing handbills of sale of personal property in said estate.

$6.00.   E. B. MOORE.

Unless it be absolutely certain that the estate is sufficient to pay all the debts, an Administrator should not pay out money except for the necessary expenses of administration, otherwise he may become personally liable.

CHAPTER III.

THE WIDOW'S INVENTORY, &C.

The widow and children of any decedent are by the Laws of Pennsylvania, entitled to retain either real or personal property belonging to the estate, to the value of Three hundred dollars.

It is made the duty of the Administrator to have this property set apart and appraised, to the widow and children, by the appraisers of the other personal property of the decedent.

The widow and children are entitled to retain Three hundred dollars, or any part of it out of any bank notes, money, stocks, judgments or other indebtedness to the decedent. Where the amount is claimed in this way there is no necessity for an appraisement.[1] The Administrator need only take from the widow a receipt as follows:

RECEIVED November 13, 1868, of Samuel C. Lewis, Administrator, of Alexander J. Wright, deceased, Three Hundred Dollars, elected to be retained by me as widow of said deceased, for the use of myself and family.

$300.   ELIZABETH D. WRIGHT.

Should personal property other than money, notes, &c., be elected to be retained by the widow and children, an inventory and appraisement is necessary.

Inventory and Appraisement of Widow's Election.

STATE OF PENNSYLVANIA, } ss.
   CHESTER COUNTY,

Henry Davis and James Long, appraisers of the personal property of Alexander J. Wright, late of Pennsbury town-

(1) Larrison's Appeal, 12 Casey, 130.

ship, County and State aforesaid, deceased, being duly affirmed, say that they will well and truly appraise and set apart the property of the said decedent to the value of Three hundred Dollars, elected to be retained by Elizabeth D. Wright, the widow of said deceased, for the use of herself and family.

Affirmed and Subscribed before me, this 20th day of October, 1868.
    Wm. Whitehead, J. P.

Henry Davis.
James Long.

Inventory and Appraisement of the Estate of the above named Alexander J. Wright, deceased, elected to be retained by Elizabeth D. Wright, widow of said deceased.

One Dozen Chairs,	$ 18	00
Table	10	00
Rocking Chair,	9	00
Bedstead,	13	00
Bedding,	15	00
Bed,	21	00
Bureau,	18	00
Wash-stand, &c.,	7	00
China-Ware,	10	00
Kitchen Stove,	8	00
Wash Tubs,	3	00
Looking-Glass,	3	00
28 yds. of Carpet,	56	50
Cow,	30	00
Book-Case,	17	50
Lot of Wood,	9	00
Cash,	63	00
	$300	00

Appraised and set apart by us, October 25, 1868.
    Henry Davis,
    James Long.

Below this should be an acceptance by the widow, as follows:

I, Elizabeth D. Wright, widow of said Alexander J. Wright, deceased, hereby elect to retain for the use of myself and family, the personal property described in the foregoing inventory and appraisement.

ELIZABETH D. WRIGHT.

October 25, 1869.

The foregoing papers, (including inventory and appraisement) must be approved by the court, and filed in the office of the Clerk of Orphans' Court.

Should there not be personal estate to the value of Three hundred Dollars, the balance of the sum can be taken from the real estate.

If the widow desires to do so, she can elect to retain the whole of Three hundred Dollars out of the real estate.

It sometimes happens, that the whole of the personal estate of the decedent, is taken by the widow to make up her Three hundred Dollars allowed by law; in such cases, the Administrator should file in the Register's office a paper showing why a general inventory is not filed.

Certificate of Administrator where the Personal Estate has been exhausted by Widow's Election.

In the matter of the Estate of Alexander J. Wright, late of Pennsbury township, Chester County, Pennsylvania, deceased.

STATE OF PENNSYLVANIA, } ss.
    CHESTER COUNTY,

Samuel C. Lewis, administrator of Alexander J. Wright, late of Pennsbury township, County and State aforesaid, deceased, being duly affirmed, says, that the whole of the personal property belonging to the estate of said deceased, was elected and retained as appraised, by Elizabeth D. Wright, widow of said decedent, for the use of herself and family in accordance with the provisions of the Act of Assembly of April 14, 1851, and for that reason no general inventory is filed in said estate.

Affirmed and Subscribed before me, this 1st day of December, 1868.
  WM. WHITEHEAD, J. P.

SAMUEL C. LEWIS,
  Administrator.

The widow has a right to retain real or personal property to the amount of Three hundred dollars from the estate of her deceased husband, whether he dies solvent or insolvent—with or without leaving a will. She is also entitled to retain Three hundred Dollars so allowed her by law, independently of her share of the estate under the intestate laws.[1]

If the decedent left no children, the Three hundred Dollars worth of property belongs to the widow absolutely.

When there is no widow, the children may retain property of the same value.

The widow is entitled to her Three hundred Dollars out of the proceeds of the sale of the real estate of the decedent in preference to a judgment creditor, in whose favor the husband had waived the benefit of the act of 1849, exempting $300 from levy and sale.[2]

The widow can claim it as against a mechanics' lien creditor.[2] She cannot claim it, however, as against a mortgage or a judgment given for purchase money.[3]

1 Compher v. Compher. 1. Casey, 31.
2 Spencer's Appeal. 3. Casey, 218.
3 Hildebrand's Appeal. 3. Wright, 133.

CHAPTER IV.

SALE OF PERSONAL PROPERTY.

Should the Administrator desire to sell personal property of the decedent, he will advertise the same by printed handbills and sell at public sale—having given twenty days notice of the time and place of sale.

The conditions of sale should be signed by the Administrator and read by the auctioneer, before commencing to sell.

Form of Conditions of Sale of Personal Property.

Conditions of Sale of the personal property of Alexander J. Wright, late of Pennsbury township, Chester county, Pennsylvania, deceased, sold at public sale, this tenth day of December, A. D., 1868, by Samuel C. Lewis, administrator, &c., of said deceased.

I. The highest and best bidder shall be the purchaser.

II. All purchases made not exceeding twenty dollars, to be paid for in cash.

III. Any person purchasing to an amount exceeding Twenty Dollars, will be allowed a credit of thirty days; and to an amount exceeding Fifty Dollars, a credit of three months, upon giving a note with approved security.

IV. No articles purchased to be removed from the premises until the conditions of sale have been complied with.

V. Any purchaser refusing to comply with the conditions of sale, will be held liable for any loss resulting from a second sale of articles purchased by him.

SAMUEL C. LEWIS,

December 10, 1868.   Administrator.

Form of Promissory Note.

$150.   PENNSBURY, December 10, 1869.

Three months after date, we, or either of us, promise to pay to Samuel C. Lewis, or order, at The National Bank of Chester County, One Hundred and Fifty $\frac{}{100}$ Dollars, without defalcation, for value received.

> 10 CENT
> INTERNAL
> REVENUE
> STAMP.

HENRY G. MORRIS.
ROBERT C. WEDD.

In accepting promissory notes, from purchasers at the sale, an Administrator must be careful to see that the person going security, *signs at the bottom of the note along with the maker, and not across the back.*

By a recent decision of the Supreme Court of Pennsylvania, the administrator could not, under such circumstances, recover against *one endorsing across the back* as security, in case the maker proved worthless. It is held that this is not a negotiable endorsement, but the promise to pay the debt of another, and must be written *under* such promise and on the face of the note.[1]

By the laws of Pennsylvania, it is made the duty of the administrator, whenever he shall sell any of the personal estate of the decedent, within thirty days thereafter, to file in the Office of the Register of Wills of the county, a true account of the articles sold, with the prices and names of purchasers.

1 Schafer v. Bank, of Easton. 9. P. F. Smith, 144.
Murray vs. McKee. 10. P. F. Smith, 35.

It not unfrequently happens that children of the decedent, desire to take certain articles of personal property at the appraisement, and without having the same sold. Where the estate is perfectly solvent, and no one will be prejudiced thereby, the Administrator can permit this to be done. He should first, however, take a receipt from such person, specifying the articles taken, with the appraised value of each attached.

Receipt for Personal Property taken at the Appraisement.

Received, November 5, 1869, of Samuel C. Lewis, administrator of Alexander J. Wright, late of Pennsbury township, Chester county, Pennsylvania, deceased, the several articles of personal property, belonging to the estate of said deceased, set forth in the following schedule, which I agree to accept at the appraised value set opposite each article respectively, amounting in the aggregate to One hundred and twenty-five Dollars. I further agree, that the said sum of One hundred and twenty-five Dollars, shall be deducted from my share or dividend of said estate in the distribution thereof, by said Administrator:

Clock,	$ 15 00
Table,	20 00
Book-Case,	14 00
½ doz. Chairs,	12 00
One Feather Bed,	16 00
15 yds. of Carpet,	30 00
Arm Chair,	12 00
Bible,	6 00
	$125 00

Witness my hand this 5th day of November, 1868.

JAMES WRIGHT.

CHAPTER V.

SALE OF REAL ESTATE FOR PAYMENT OF DEBTS.

Whenever it shall satisfactorily appear to the Administrator, that the personal estate is insufficient to pay all just debts and expenses of administration, he should apply at once by petition to the Orphans' Court, for authority to sell the real estate for that purpose.

Form of Petition for Sale of Real Estate for Payment of Debts.

To the Honorable, the Judges of the Orphans' Court of Chester county, Pennsylvania:

The petition of Samuel C. Lewis, administrator of Alexander J. Wright, late of Pennsbury township, Chester county, Pennsylvania, deceased—

Respectfully represents:

That the said Alexander J. Wright, died on or about the twentieth day of September, A. D. 1868, intestate, leaving to survive him a widow, Elizabeth D. Wright, and four children—James, William, Mary and Thomas—the last being a minor, and having for his Guardian, William Parker, of said county:

The petitioner further represents that the said Alexander J. Wright died seized of and in certain real estate, situate in said county, a description of which is hereunto annexed.

That the personal estate of the decedent is insufficient for the payment of his debts, as appears by an inventory and appraisement of all the personal estate of the decedent, and a just and true account of all his debts, which have come to the knowledge of the Administrator, herewith exhibited.

The petitioner therefore prays the Court to order the sale of said real estate, for the payment of the debts of said decedent.

And he will, &c.

January 3, 1869.

SAMUEL C. LEWIS,
Administrator.

To this should be attached a certificate from the Register of Wills, as to the amount of the personal estate of the decedent.

Form of Register's Certificate.

STATE OF PENNSYLVANIA, } ss.
   CHESTER COUNTY,

I, Hampton S. Thomas, Register for the Probate of Wills and granting Letters of Administration, &c., in and for the county aforesaid, do certify that the amount of the personal property of Alexander J. Wright, late of Pennsbury township, in said county, deceased, as appears by the inventory and appraisement of the same filed in this office, is Six thousand and ninety-five $\frac{—}{100}$ ($6,095.) Dollars.

[SEAL]   Given under my hand, and the seal of said office, at West Chester, this second day of January, A. D. 1869.

HAMPTON S. THOMAS,
Register, &c.

A statement of all the debts of the said Alexander J. Wright, deceased.

Caleb Brinton, Mortgage,	4,000	00
4 years Interest,	960	00
David Meconkey, Judg't Bond,	1,900	00
Wm. McClellan, Prom. Note,	725	00
James & Devoe, Book Account,	230	75
David D. Nelson, " "	150	00
Dr. John Taylor, Physician's Bill,	85	00
Wm. Hoofman, Undertaker,	120	00
Hugh Maxwell, Bond,	450	00
State and County Taxes for 1868,	104	75
Benjamin Carter, Due Bill,	82	50
James Reily, Wages,	68	00
Bridget Kelly, "	30	00
Expenses of Administration,	250	00
	$9,156	00

Statement of all the Real Estate of the said Alexander J. Wright, deceased.

No. 1.—Messuage and tract of land situate in Pennsbury township, Chester county, bounded by lands of Robert Ralston, James Walker, John C. Pomeroy, Richard Kennedy and others, and containing two hundred and twenty-five acres, more or less.

No. 2.—A tract of woodland situate in Pocopson township, in said county, bounded by lands of William Dowlin, Alexander McClure, Charles Gregler and others, and containing ten acres, more or less.

Following this, should be an affidavit of two disinterested persons, as to the value of the real estate, so that the Court may be informed with reference to the amount of security it should require of the Administrator.

STATE OF PENNSYLVANIA, } ss.
   CHESTER COUNTY,

Lewis Parker and Henry Beaver, being duly affirmed, say, that they are well acquainted with the above described real estate of Alexander J. Wright, deceased, and are of opinion that the same would sell at a cash sale as follows, viz: Tract No. 1—For the sum of Twenty thousand Dollars. Tract No. 2—For the sum of Seven hundred and fifty Dollars, and that they have no interest whatever in said estate.

Affirmed and subscribed before me, } LEWIS PARKER.
   this 2d day of January, 1869.
        WM. WHITEHEAD, J. P. } HENRY BEAVER.

The Administrator should then make the following affidavit:

STATE OF PENNSYLVANIA, } ss.
   CHESTER COUNTY,

Samuel C. Lewis being duly affirmed, says, that the facts set forth in the foregoing petition are true, and the exhibits appended thereto, are respectively, a correct statement of all the personal estate of the said deceased, as well as of all his real estate, and a true account of all the debts of the said decedent, which have come to his knowlege, as he verily believes.

Affirmed and Subscribed beforem e, } SAMUEL C. LEWIS,
   this 3d day of January, 1869.
        WM. WHITEHEAD, J. P. } Administrator.

The Petition, Certificate of Register, Statement of Debts, Description of Real Estate, Affidavit or Appraisers and of the Administrator, should all be fastened together (usually on the same sheet of paper) ready for presentation to the Court.

The names of two persons must, at the time of presenting the petition, be suggested to the Court as sureties of the Administrator. They should be owners of real estate, and worth, clear of encumbrances, double the amount named in the bond.

Form of Bond of Administrator for Sale of Real Estate.

KNOW ALL MEN BY THESE PRESENTS, That we, Samuel C. Lewis, administrator of Alexander J. Wright, late of Pennsbury township, Chester county, Pennsylvania, deceased, Thomas R. Perkins and Samuel B. Dickey, all of the County and State aforesaid, are held and firmly bound unto the Commonwealth of Pennsylvania, in the sum of Fifty-four thousand Dollars, lawful money of the United States of America, to be paid to the said Commonwealth, to which payment, well and truly to be made, we bind ourselves, our Heirs, Executors, Administrators, and every of them, jointly and severally, firmly by these presents. Sealed with our seals, and dated the fifteenth day of January, in the year of our Lord, one thousand eight hundred and sixty-nine.

WHEREAS, at an Orphans' Court, held and kept at West Chester, for the County of Chester, the sixth day of January, A. D., 1869, before the Honorable William Butler, and his associates, Judges, present, the above bounden, Samuel C. Lewis, administrator, &c., as aforesaid, was ordered to sell the Real Estate of said deceased, as in said order more particularly specified, he having given security in the above mentioned sum.

NOW THE CONDITION OF THIS OBLIGATION IS SUCH, That if the above bounden, Samuel C. Lewis, administrator, &c., as aforesaid, shall faithfully appropriate the proceeds of such sale according to his duties, then this obligation to be void, or else to be and remain in full force and virtue.

Sealed and delivered in the presence of
JOHN FOSTER.
THOMAS HUGHES.

SAMUEL C. LEWIS. [L. S.]
THOMAS R. PERKINS, [L. S.]
SAMUEL B. DICKEY. [L. S.]

A sale of real estate by order of Orphans' Court for the payment of debts of the decedent, must be public.

Twenty days notice must be given by advertisement in a newspaper published in the county, if there be one, or if there be none, then in the adjoining county; and also by printed handbills posted in the most public places in the vicinity of the sale, for the same length of time.

The Administrator should be careful to see that the real estate is well described in the advertisements, so that it may sell to the best advantage. Courts will set aside a sale upon exceptions, where inadequacy of price is shown, by reason of a failure to properly describe the premises.

It has been thought not out of place, to insert here, a form of advertisement of real estate, embodying many of the points proper to be mentioned in describing it.

Form of Advertisement of Real Estate.

PUBLIC SALE OF VALUABLE REAL ESTATE.

Pursuant to an order of the Orphans' Court of Chester county, Pennsylvania, will be sold at public sale, on the premises, in Pennsbury township, in said county, on Wednesday, the 16th day of February, A. D. 1869, the following described real estate, late of Alexander J. Wright, deceased, to wit:

A valuable farm situate in Pennsbury township, on the road leading from West Chester to Wilmington, about eight miles from West Chester, and three miles from the thriving village of Hamorton, bounded by lands of Robert Ralston, James Walker, John C. Pomeroy, Richard Kennedy and others, and containing two hundred and twenty-five acres, more or less.

The improvements are a large and convenient stone mansion house, seventy by seventy-five feet, two stories and a half; four rooms and a hall on the first floor, eight rooms on the second, and four in the attic; the house has two piazzas, and is enclosed in a fine lawn. There is a stone kitchen attached, twenty by sixteen feet; stone spring house over a never-failing spring of water; stone smoke house, frame wood house, ice house, hen house, &c., &c. A large stone barn of the most substantial character and completely furnished—one hundred and twenty feet by sixty feet, and twenty feet high to the square—with two large threshing floors; good granaries and first-rate stabling, straw house, carriage house, hog house and corn crib attached, all in good repair.

The land is in a high state of cultivation, having been heavily limed all over within the last two years; is divided into convenient fields, with water in each field except one, and all under good fence. The farm is well adapted for grazing and farming purposes; about forty-five acres of the property is woodland, well set with oak, hickory, chestnut and other timber. There are two fine apple orchards in good bearing order, as well as a choice variety of cherry, peach, plum and other fruit trees.

This property is half a mile from "Summit" Station on The Philadelphia and Baltimore Central Railroad, and one mile from "Pennelton" Station, on The Philadelphia and West Chester Railroad; is located in one of the best neighhoods in Chester county, and convenient to places of public worship of all denominations, schools, stores, mills, &c., &c.

Persons desiring to view the premises, will please call on Silas Walton, residing thereon.

Sale to commence at 2 o'clock, P. M. Conditions made known at sale, by

SAMUEL C. LEWIS,

January 16th, 1869.   Administrator.

At the time of sale, the conditions should be publicly announced. They should set forth fully and clearly, the terms upon which the property is to be sold, and be signed by the Administrator.

Form of Conditions of Sale.

CONDITIONS OF SALE of a messuage and tract of land, situate in the township of Pennsbury, in the County of Chester, and State of Pennsylvania, bounded by lands of Robert Ralston, James Walker, John C. Pomeroy, Richard Kennedy and others, containing two hundred and twenty-five acres, more or less, with the appurtenances, late the estate of Alexander J. Wright, deceased, exposed to sale the sixteenth day of February, Anno Domini, one thousand eight hundred and sixty-nine. By order of the Orphans' Court of said county.

1. The highest and best bidder to be the purchaser, the vendor reserving one open bid. If any dispute shall arise as to the last or best bidder, the property may, at the option of the vendor, be put up again at a former bid.

2. All grain in the ground is reserved, with privilege to the present owner or owners, to enter upon the premises in the proper seasons, and care for, cut, stow, thresh and haul it away, he or they leaving the straw upon the premises.

3. Immediately upon the property being struck down, the purchaser shall pay the vendor ten per cent. of the purchase money, or give a note for the amount thereof, with approved security, payable in thirty days; the purchaser shall also enter into an obligation, with approved security, conditioned for the payment of the balance of the purchase money on the first day of April, A. D., 1869, and for a faithful compliance in all respects, with all the conditions of the sale.

4. A deed for all the rights, title, and interest, of the said Alexander J. Wright, in said real estate, will be executed and delivered to the purchaser, (he having complied with all the conditions of sale,) on the first day of April next. All necessary instruments of writing, and the proper stamps, to be at the expense of the purchaser.

5. Any person to whom the said tract of land shall be fairly struck down, and who shall refuse to comply with these conditions, shall be held liable for all damage resulting from such refusal, and shall not be entitled to any benefit of a subsequent sale; but the vendor shall have the option to consider the above percentage, paid or secured to be paid, as

damages fairly liquidated and ascertained by the parties, for the breach of the contract.

SAMUEL C. LEWIS,
Administrator.

Printed, or written, upon the same sheet with the conditions of sale, it is customary to add an obligation or agreement to be entered into by the purchaser and his sureties, for the payment of the balance of the purchase money, and a compliance with the conditions of sale.

Form of Agreement with Purchaser.

I, George Williams, of the township of Londongrove, in the county of Chester, Pennsylvania, do acknowledge that the within mentioned tract of land was fairly struck down to me, at my bid, for the sum of Twenty thousand four hundred and twenty-five Dollars. And I covenant and agree, to and with, the said Samuel C. Lewis, administrator of Alexander J. Wright, deceased, to pay the said purchase money according to said conditions, and in all respects to comply with the same.

Witness my hand and seal this sixteenth day of February, A. D. 1869.

Signed and Delivered in
the presence of
    JAMES TURNER.
    THOMAS SPEAKMAN.

[5 Cent INTERNAL Revenue STAMP.]

GEORGE WILLIAMS.

We, John S. Gibbons and Henry G. Thomas, the subscribers hereto, covenant and agree, to and with the said Samuel C. Lewis, administrator of Alexander J. Wright, deceased, for a valuable consideration, that the above named George Williams, purchaser as aforesaid, shall comply with the foregoing conditions of sale, and pay the said purchase money according to the said conditions, or in case of his failure, that we will pay said purchase money for him.

Witness our hands and seals, this sixteenth day of February, A. D. 1869.

Signed and Delivered in
in the presence of
  JAMES TURNER,
  THOMAS SPEAKMAN.

JOHN S. GIBBONS, [L. S.]

HENRY G. THOMAS, [L. S.]

The usual course is to require a *cash* payment of say ten per cent. of the purchase money, and the balance in thirty, sixty or ninety days. This can always be changed, however, to suit the peculiar circumstances of the case; taking care always that enough is paid down to cover any loss that might result from the failure of the purchaser to make the required payments. Credit should not be allowed in any case, beyond the time fixed for making title to the purchaser, and giving possession of the premises.

It has been decided that an Administrator having given legal notice of the time and place of the sale of real estate, in pursuance of an order of the Orphans' Court, and not being then able to effect a sale, may adjourn the same to a day less remote than twenty days.[1]

Should the Administrator fail to sell at all, he must make return of the fact to the court, and, if it is desired, an *alias* order can subsequently be directed to issue.

Form of Return where Land is Unsold.

TO THE HONORABLE, THE JUDGES WITHIN NAMED :

I, Samuel C. Lewis, administrator, &c., of Alexander J. Wright, deceased, do
              Respectfully report :
                          That having given due public notice of the time and place of sale, in accordance with the provisions of the 54th Section of the Act of Assembly, en-

[1] Gillespie's Estate. 10 Watts, 300.

titled "An act relating to Orphans' Court," passed the 29th day of March, A. D., 1832, I exposed the within mentioned real estate to public sale, on the Sixteenth day of February, A. D., 1869, but that the same remains unsold for want of buyers.

          SAMUEL C. LEWIS,
February 25, 1868.   Administrator.

Return to an Order of Sale.

TO THE HONORABLE, THE JUDGES WITHIN NAMED:

I, Samuel C. Lewis, administrator, &c., &c., of Alexander J. Wright, deceased, do
      Respectfully report:
         That having given due public notice of the time and place of sale, in accordance with the provisions of the 54th Section of the Act of Assembly, entitled "An act relating to Orphans' Courts," passed the 29th day of March, A. D., 1832, I exposed the within mentioned real estate to public sale, on the Sixteenth day of February, 1869, and sold the same to George Williams, of said county, for the sum of Twenty-one thousand five hundred ($21,500) Dollars, he being the best bidder, and that the highest price bidden for the same.

Which sale I pray may be confirmed by this Court.

          SAMUEL C. LEWIS,
February 25th, 1869.   Administrator.

CHAPTER VI.

DEED FOR REAL ESTATE OF DECEDENT.

Upon the confirmation of the sale by the Court, the Administrator should have a deed properly prepared, executed and stamped, ready for delivery, at the time mentioned in the conditions of sale.

Form of Deed from Administrator, for Real Estate sold by Order of Orphans' Court, for Payment of Debts.

THIS INDENTURE, made the thirty-first day of March, A. D., one thousand eight hundred and sixty-nine, between Samuel C. Lewis, administrator, &c., of Alexander J. Wright, late of Pennsbury township, Chester county, Pennsylvania, deceased, of the one part, and George Williams, of Londongrove township, County and State aforesaid, of the other part:

WHEREAS, at an Orphans' Court held at West Chester, in and for the County of Chester, and State of Pennsylvania, the sixth day of January, A. D., one thousand eight hundred and sixty-nine, upon the petition of Samuel C. Lewis, the Administrator aforesaid, setting forth that the personal estate of the said deceased was insufficient for the payment of his debts, and praying the court to direct a sale of the real estate of the said decedent, hereinafter described, for that purpose, it was ordered and decreed by the said court, that the premises hereinafter described, should be sold for the purposes aforesaid, and report of the proceedings thereof be made to the next term thereof, after such sale.

AND WHEREAS, in pursuance of which said order, the said

Samuel C. Lewis, administrator, &c., as aforesaid, after having given due public notice of the time and place of sale, in accordance with the 54th section of the act approved 29th day of March, A. D., 1832, did, on the Sixteenth day of February, A. D., One thousand eight hundred and sixty-nine, expose the said real estate hereinafter described, to public sale, and sold the same to the said George Williams, for the sum of Twenty-one thousand five hundred Dollars, he being the best bidder, and that the highest price bidden for the same; which sale, on report thereof made to said court, was, on the Twenty-fifth day of February following, by them confirmed. And it was considered and adjudged by the said court, that the same should be and remain firm and stable forever, as by the records and proceedings of the said court, will appear.

Now this Indenture Witnesseth, That the said Samuel C. Lewis, administrator, &c., as aforesaid, for and in consideration of the said sum of Twenty-one thousand five hundred Dollars, to him in hand paid by the said George Williams, at and before the sealing and delivery hereof, the receipt whereof he doth hereby acknowledge, and thereof acquit and forever discharge the said George Williams, his heirs, executors and administrators, by these presents, has granted, bargained, sold, released and confirmed, and by these presents doth grant, bargain, sell, release and confirm unto the said George Williams, and to his heirs and assigns, all that certain messuage and tract of land, situate in Pennsbury township, Chester county, Pennsylvania, bounded and described as follows: Beginning [here describe property.] Containing Two hundred and twenty-five acres of land, more or less, with the appurtenances. (It being the same premises which Richard L. Walters and wife by their Indenture, dated the First day of April, A. D., One thousand eight hundred and thirty-one, and recorded in the office of the Recorder of Deeds, of Chester county, Pennsylvania, in Deed Book B. 3, Vol. 296, page 62, granted and conveyed to the said Alexander J. Wright, in fee simple.)

TOGETHER with all and singular the improvements, houses, buildings, barns, stables, ways, woods, waters, water courses, rights, liberties, privileges, hereditaments, and appurtenances, whatsoever thereunto belonging, or in anywise appertaining, and the reversions and remainders, rents, issues, and profits, thereof; and also all the estate, right, title, interest, property, claim, and demand whatsoever, of the said Alexander J. Wright, at and immediately before the time of his decease, in law or equity, or otherwise howsoever, of, in, to, or out of the same.

To HAVE AND TO HOLD the said messuage and tract of land, and premises hereby granted, or mentioned or intended so to be, with the appurtenances, unto the said George Williams, his heirs and assigns, to the only proper use and behoof of the said George Williams, his heirs and assigns forever. AND the said Samuel C. Lewis, administrator, aforesaid, for himself, his heirs, executors and administrators, doth covenant, promise, grant and agree, to and with the said George Williams, his heirs and assigns, by these presents, that he, the said Samuel C. Lewis, has not heretofore done or committed any act, matter, or thing whatsoever, whereby the premises hereby granted, or any part thereof is, are, or shall, or may be impeached, charged or encumbered, in title, charge, estate, or otherwise howsoever.

Signed, Sealed and Delivered in presence of (an internal revenue stamp of the value of $21 50/100 having been first affixed and canceled.)
ROBT. L. MCCLELLAN.
ARCHIMEDES ROBB.

IN WITNESS WHEREOF, The said party of the first part, has hereunto set his hand and seal, the day and year first above written.
SAMUEL C. LEWIS, [L. S.]

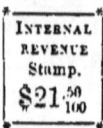

STATE OF PENNSYLVANIA, } ss.
CHESTER COUNTY,

On this Thirty-first day of March, A. D., 1869, before me a Justice of the Peace, in and for said State and County, personally appeared the above named Samuel C. Lewis, administrator as aforesaid, and acknowledged the above written indenture to be his act and deed, and desired that the same might be recorded as such, according to law.

In testimony whereof, I have hereunto set my hand and seal the day and year above written.

WM. WHITEHEAD, [L. S.]
J. P.

CHAPTER VII.

PAYMENT OF DEBTS OF DECEDENT.

No Administrator can be compelled to pay any debts of the decedent, except such as are by law preferred, in the order of payment to rents, until one year be fully elapsed from the granting of the administration of the estate.

The order of paying the debts of a decedent, is as follows :

1. Funeral expenses, medicine furnished, medical attendance during the last illness of the decedent, and servants' wages, not exceeding one year.
2. Rents, not exceeding one year.
3. All other debts (not secured by judgment.)
4. Debts due the Commonwealth.

This means, of course, out of the *personal* estate of the decedent. The real estate is always first subject to the payment of the liens upon it.[1]

If the real estate is insufficient to pay the liens, and there is a fund arising from sale of personal estate, the lien creditors can only look to the personal property after exhausting the real estate; they are then entitled to a *pro rata* distribution with other creditors not of record.

A claim for wages, ceases to be a "preferred debt" wherever the creditor has accepted from the decedent, a note or due bill for the same, payable at a future day, with interest.[1]

1 Wade's Appeal. 5 Casey, 329.
  Johnston's Estate. 9 Casey, 513.
2 Silver *v.* Williams. 17 Sergeant & Rawle, 293.

A claim for wages "not exceeding a year," is not confined to services during the *last* year of the decedent's life.[1]

Funeral expenses cannot be paid out of the proceeds of real estate, where such real estate is insufficient to pay the liens.

Judge Woodward, in deciding this point, remarks: "It has been correctly said, that a man dying the owner of ample real estate, might have to be buried at public expense as a pauper, if he had no personal property, and his realty was encumbered by liens to its full value."[2] Singular as this may appear to many, it is however, a judgment of the court, not yet changed or modified, and must govern Administrators in their conduct.

If there are not sufficient assets in the hands of the Administrator, to pay all the debts of the estate, the safer course is for him to file his account, within the time prescribed by law, and petition the court for an Auditor to report distribution.

Any creditor may petition for an Auditor to report distribution.

Form of Petition for an Auditor to make Distribution.

To the Honorable, the Judges of the Orphans' Court of Chester County, Pennsylvania;

The petition of the undersigned—

Respectfully represents:

That Samuel C. Lewis, administrator of Alexander J. Wright, late of Pennsbury township, in said State and County, deceased, has settled an account of his administration of the estate of said decedent, which was confirmed *nisi* by this court, on the ninth day of March last, by which it appears that there is a balance of Four thousand two hundred ($4,200) Dollars belonging to said estate, remaining in the hand of said Administrator.

That your petitioner is interested in said estate, and there-

---

[1] Martin's Appeal.   9 Casey, 395.
[2] Wade's Appeal.   5 Casey, 329.

fore prays the Court, to appoint an auditor, to make distribution of said balance, amongst the parties entitled thereto.
And he will, &c.

March 30, 1869. LEVI G. ALLISON.

In paying off a judgment bond, given by the decedent, the Administrator should require the instrument to be surrendered, and take a receipt, upon the back of the bond, for debt interest and costs; and at the same time, procure from the creditor, a direction to enter satisfaction upon the record.

Form of Direction to Satisfy Judgment.

DAVID MECONKEY, } In the Common Pleas of Chester County, Pennsylvania. See Judgment entered the 15th day of March, A. D., 1861, in Judgment Docket A. 2., page 396. Debt $750.00
vs.
ALEXANDER J. WRIGHT.

To ALFRED RUPERT, ESQ.,
PROTHONOTARY:

SIR: The payment of the debt, interest and costs of the above recited judgment, is hereby acknowledged, and you will please mark the same satisfied of record.

Yours, &c.

Witnesses Present.
LEVI PRESTON.
HIRAM HALL.

DAVID MECONKEY,
Plaintiff.
April 3d, 1869.

In paying off a mortgage, the Administrator should require a surrender of both the bond and mortgage, and take a receipt, upon the back of the bond, for debt, interest, and costs.

The mortgage should be satisfied by the mortgagee going personally to the Recorder's office, as this course is attended with the least expense.

When, upon the other hand, however, the Administrator is receiving the amount of a judgment, in favor of the decedent, he should not forget to take the entry fee (if paid by the decedent,) and also the Prothonotary's fee, for the entry of satisfaction.

In the case of a mortgage, he is entitled to receive the cost of recording, (if it has been paid by decedent) and fee for entering satisfaction.

The fee for entering satisfaction of a judgment, is twenty cents; of a mortgage, sixty cents.

CHAPTER VIII.

ADMINISTRATION ACCOUNT.

By the terms of his bond, an Administrator is required to file an account of his administration, within one year from the time of issuing letters.

This account is filed in the office of the Register of Wills. The fee for filing the same should be included in the account, in the credits of the Administrator.

Form of an Administration Account.

An Account of the administration of Samuel C. Lewis, administrator, &c., of Alexander J. Wright, late of Pennsbury township, Chester county, deceased:

The Accountant charges himself as follows, viz:		
To amount of inventory and appraisement of personal property filed,	6,095	00
To advance on sale of personal property, above appraisement,	280	00
To cash received from Abner Davis, since filing inventory,	130	00
Cash received from Jacob L. Jefferis, *book account omitted in inventory,	35	00
	$6,540	00

The Accountant claims credit as follows, viz :		
By cash paid for letters of administration, &c.,	3	95
By cash paid for stamps on inventory and bond,	4	50
By cash paid appraisers personal property,	2	00
By cash paid H. S. Evans, advertising and printing,	9	50
By cash paid Joseph G. King, auctioneer,	5	00
By cash paid John Jackson, clerk of sale,	3	00
By cash paid Wm. Whitehead, Esq., affidavits,	1	50
By cash paid Wm. Hoofman, funeral expenses,	120	00
By cash paid Dr. John Taylor, physician's bill,	85	00
By cash paid James Riley, labor,	68	00
By cash paid Bridget Kelley, wages,	30	00
By cash paid Register passing this account,	10	30
By cash paid James J. Williams, counsel fees,	75	00
By Compensation to accountant,	325	00
Balance due the esstate,	5,797	25
	$6,540	00

Errors Excepted, }   SAMUEL C. LEWIS,
January 12th, 1869. }   Administrator.

No general rule can be established with respect to the commissions to be allowed to Administrators. The ordinary allowance in Pennsylvania, however, is five per cent. upon personal property.[1]

[1] Gable's Appeal. 12 Casey, 395.

And upon sales of real estate, the later decisions have recognized three per cent. as a proper allowance.[2]

Where the amount of the estate is small, the collections made in small sums and with considerable personal trouble, the compensation may exceed what we have mentioned. On the other hand, where the value of the estate is very great, and far exceeds the debts, and the Administrator has had little trouble or hazard, the money being paid in large sums, a smaller per cent. has been deemed sufficient.

2 Harper's Appeal.   5 Wright, 49,
  Snyder's Appeal.   4 P. F. Smith, 69.

CHAPTER IX.

DISTRIBUTION OF THE ESTATE.

Where an Administrator has money in his hands belonging to a distributee, whose residence is known, it is the duty of the Administrator to give notice of his readiness to pay the money, and hold it subject to the owner's demand.

When the residence of one entitled to share in the distribution is unknown, and cannot be ascertained upon reasonable inquiry, the fund may be retained by the Administrator in his hands, for any period not exceeding one year, and should then be invested.[1]

It has been decided in Pennsylvania, that where the residence of a distributee was unknown, and could not be ascertained by reasonable inquiry, an executor was chargeable with interest after twelve months from the settlement of his account.[2]

In making distribution of an estate, the Administrator should require from those entitled to distributive shares, a refunding bond, with two sureties, in double the amount of the share paid over. If an Administrator neglects to take such refunding bond, he is personally liable for claims subsequently recovered against the estate.[3]

Form of Refunding Bond.

KNOW ALL MEN BY THESE PRESENTS, That We, James Wright, of Pennsbury township, Chester county, Pennsyl-

1 Walthour's, Adms. v. Walthour's Adms.   2 Grant, 102.
2 Campbell v. Reed.   12 Harris, 500.
3 Musser v. Oliver.   9 Harris, 367.

vania, one of the heirs and distributees of Alexander J. Wright, late of said township, deceased, David L. Ross and Levi Dilworth, all of said County and State, are held and firmly bound unto Samuel C. Lewis, administrator, &c., of said deceased, in the sum of Three thousand six hundred ($3,600) Dollars, lawful money of the United States, to be paid to the said Samuel C. Lewis, administrator, as aforesaid, his certain attorney, executors, administrators, and assigns, to which payment well and truly to be made, we do bind ourselves, our heirs, executors, and administrators, firmly by these presents; Sealed with our seals, dated the fifteenth day of June, A. D., one thousand eight hundred and sixty-nine.

WHEREAS, the said James Wright has this day had and received from Samuel C. Lewis, administrator of Alexander J. Wright, late of Pennsbury township, Chester county, Pennsylvania, deceased, the sum of Eighteen hundred Dollars, being his share of the estate of the said deceased, as appears by the account of the said Samuel C. Lewis, administrator, as aforesaid, filed in the Register's office of Chester county, Pennsylvania, on the 12th day of January, A. D. 1869.

NOW THE CONDITION OF THIS OBLIGATION IS SUCH, That if any debt or demand shall hereafter be recovered against the estate of the said Alexander J. Wright, deceased, or otherwise be duly made to appear, and the said James Wright shall refund a rateable part of such debt or demand, and of the costs and charges attending the recovery of the same, then this obligation shall be void, or else shall be and remain in full force and virtue.

Signed, Sealed and Delivered in presence of
EVAN T. LEWIS.
JAMES MODE.

JAMES WRIGHT, [L. S.]

DAVID L. ROSS, [L. S.]

LEVI DILWORTH, [L. S.]

It is also proper that the Administrator, upon paying over to the legatees their respective shares, should take from each, a release of all matters growing out of the administration of the estate.

Form of a Release from Heirs to the Administrator.

KNOW ALL MEN BY THESE PRESENTS, That I, James Wright, of Pennsbury township, Chester county, Pennsylvania, one of the children of Alexander J. Wright, late of Pennsbury township, County and State aforesaid, deceased, do hereby acknowledge that I have this day had and received from Samuel C. Lewis, administrator, &c., of said Alexander J. Wright, deceased, the sum of Eighteen hundred Dollars, being in full payment and satisfaction of my share of the estate, real and personal, of said deceased, as appears by the account of the said Samuel C. Lewis, administrator as aforesaid, filed in the Register's Office of Chester County, Pennsylvania, on the 12th day of January, A. D., 1869.

In consideration whereof, I do hereby remise, release, quit claim, and forever discharge the said Samuel C. Lewis, administrator as aforesaid, his executors and administrators, of and from the said share or shares, dividend or dividends aforesaid, and of and from all actions, suits, payments, accounts, reckonings, claims and demands, for or by reason thereof, or of any other act, matter, cause or thing whatsoever, from said estate or on account of the administration thereof, to the date of these presents.

In witness whereof, I have hereunto set my hand and seal, this fifteenth day of June, A. D., one thousand eight hundred and sixty-nine.

Signed, sealed, and delivered
in presence of
    EVAN T. LEWIS.
    JAMES MODE.

JAMES WRIGHT. [L. S.]

STATE OF PENNSYLVANIA, } ss.
CHESTER COUNTY,

On this fifteenth day of June, before me, a Justice of the Peace in and for said State and County, personally appeared the above named James Wright, and acknowledged the foregoing release to be his act and deed, and desired that the same might be recorded as such, according to law.

In witness whereof I have hereunto set my hand and seal, the day and year aforesaid.

Wm. Whitehead, [L. S.]
J. P.

The release should be acknowledged, as above, before a Justice of the Peace, and recorded in the office for recording deeds.

Whenever a married woman, of lawful age, is entitled to a legacy or distributive share, the proceeds of real or personal estate, she can can give a refunding bond for that purpose, or execute a release for the same, with like effect, as if she were sole and unmarried.[1]

[1] Act of 11th April, 1856.   Pamphlet laws, 315.

CHAPTER X.

COLLATERAL INHERITANCE TAX.

Collateral inheritance tax is payable upon all estates, real, personal, and mixed, passing to persons who do not stand in the relation to the decedent of father, mother, husband, wife, children, and lineal descendants.

An estate passing to a grandmother, is subject to collateral inheritance tax.[1]

Estates devised to the wife or widow of the testator's son, are not liable to collateral inheritance tax.

Estates valued at less than Two hundred and fifty Dollars, are not subject to collateral inheritance tax.

The Register usually takes from the Administrator a bond with two sufficient sureties, conditioned for the payment of the collateral tax, as well as any interest charged upon the same.

Form of Bond for Collateral Tax.

KNOW ALL MEN BY THESE PRESENTS, That we, Joseph J. Adams, administrator, &c., of Levi Evans, late of West Whiteland township, Chester county, Pennsylvania, deceased, Robert D. Painter, and Henry W. Gray, are held and bound unto the Commonwealth of Pennsylvania, in the sum of One thousand Dollars, to be paid to the said Commonwealth, to which payment well and truly to be made, we bind ourselves, jointly and severally, for and in the whole, our heirs, executors and administrators firmly by these pres-

[1] McDowell *v.* Addams, *et al.* 9 Wright, 435.

ents. Sealed with our seals, dated the tenth day of May, in the year of our Lord one thousand eight hundred and sixty-nine.

THE CONDITIONS OF THIS OBLIGATION ARE SUCH, That if the above bounden Joseph J. Adams, administrator, &c., of Levi Evans, late of the township of West Whiteland, in said county, deceased, does well and truly pay or cause to be paid to the Register of Wills, of the county of Chester, all collateral inheritance tax to which the estate of the said Levi Evans, deceased, may be subject to the payment of under the existing laws of this Commonwealth, together with such interest as may be charged upon the same under the laws aforesaid, then this obligation to be void, or else to be and remain in full force and virtue.

Sealed and Delivered in the presence of
  THOMAS BELL,
  ISAAC ACKER.

JOSEPH J. ADAMS, [L. S.]
ROBERT D. PAINTER, [L. S.]
HENRY W. GRAY, [L. S.]

If the estate is subject to collateral inheritance tax, the Administrator should inform the Register of the fact, at the time of taking out letters of administration that he may then appoint a Collateral Appraiser, and thus save the trouble of making a separate appraisement.

The usual practice is to appoint as Collateral Appraiser, one of the appraisers of the personal estate of the decedent.

Form of Appointment of Collateral Appraiser.

IN THE MATTER OF THE ESTATE OF Levi Evans, late of the township of West Whiteland, in the county of Chester, deceased, which estate is subject to the payment of a collateral inheritance tax, by the laws of the Commonwealth of Pennsylvania, I, Hampton S. Thomas, Register of Wills in the county of Chester, hereby appoint Henry W. Davis, of the township of West Whiteland, in said county, Appraiser of the estate of the above named Levi Evans, deceased, for the purpose of putting a fair valuation on the real estate of said deceased, making a fair and conscionable appraisement of the personal estate of said deceased, assessing and fixing the present cash value of all annuities and life estates growing out of said estate, and generally for performing all duties imposed upon such Appraiser by the two several Acts of the General Assembly of the Commonwealth of Pennsylvania, one approved April 10th, 1849, entitled "An Act to create a Sinking Fund, and to provide for the gradual and certain extinguishment of the debt of the Commonwealth;" the other approved March 11th, 1850, entitled "An Act relating to Collateral Inheritance."

[SEAL OF REGISTER.] In Witness whereof, I have hereunto subscribed my name, and affixed the seal of said office, at West Chester, this 10th day of May, A. D., 1869.

HAMPTON S. THOMAS,
Register.

Before entering upon his duties the Appraiser must be affirmed or sworn as follows:

STATE OF PENNSYLVANIA, } ss.
CHESTER COUNTY,

Henry W. Davis, appointed by the Register of Wills of said County, being duly affirmed according to law, declares and says that he will put a fair valuation on the real estate of Levi Evans, late of the township of West Whiteland, deceased, and make a fair and conscionable appraisement of the personal estate of said decedent, and assess and fix the present cash value of all annuities and life estates growing out of said estate, and that he will well and truly, and without prejudice or partiality, value and appraise the goods, chattels and credits of said deceased, and in all respects perform his duty as appraiser, to the best of his skill and judgment.

Affirmed and Subscribed this 16th day of May, 1869.
    WM. WHITEHEAD,
            J. P.
} HENRY W. DAVIS.

The inventory and appraisement, made by the Collateral Appraiser, should include *the real estate*, as well as the personal property of the decedent, differing, in this regard, from the general inventory filed by the Administrator.

Form of Collateral Inventory.

Inventory and Appraisement of the Real and Personal Estate of Levi Evans, late of West Whiteland township, Chester county, Pennsylvania, deceased, said estate being subject to collateral inheritance tax.

Amount of personal property of said deceased, as specifically set forth in the general inventory and appraisement of the same, filed in the Register's office.	5,100 00
149 Acres of land, situate in West Whiteland township, Chester county, Pennsylvania, bounded by lands of Jacob Fetters, Joseph Hawley, Edward A. Price, Joseph B. Thomas, and others, at $100 per acre.	14,900 00
	$20,000 00

Appraised by me, this Thirtieth day of May, A. D., 1869.
            HENRY W. DAVIS.

ADMINISTRATOR. 53

The inventory, when completed, should be attached to the certificate of appointment and affidavit, and returned to the office of Register of Wills.

The Administrator may appeal from the valuation made by the Collateral Appraiser, of the *personal* property of the decedent, if he deems it incorrect. But with the valuation made of the *real* estate, he has nothing whatever to do. It belongs to the *heirs* alone, to question the valuation of the real estate.

The Administrator has no right to pay the collateral tax upon the real estate, out of the proceeds of personal property. The heirs must pay the collateral tax upon the real estate.[1]

The fees of Collateral Appraisers, in Philadelphia, and in the cities and seats of justice, is one dollar per day; in the counties of the Commonwealth, one dollar and fifty cents per day.

The collateral inheritance tax in Pennsylvania, is, by the Act of 22d of April, 1846, five per cent.

If the collateral inheritance tax is paid to the Register within three months, from *the death of the decedent*, a discount of five per cent., upon such tax is allowed. If the tax is not paid *within one year*, from the death of the decedent, twelve per cent. per annum, interest upon such tax, will be charged. This interest upon the tax, will be computed from one year from the date of the death of the decedent.

Where, from claims made upon the estate, litigation, or other unavoidable cause or delay, the estate of a decedent, or a part of it, cannot be settled up at the end of a year from the death, *six* per cent. interest only, will be charged upon the collateral inheritance tax, from the end of such year.

It is the duty of the Administrator or Executor, however, where a part of an estate cannot be settled up within the year, to estimate the amount involved in difficulties, and pay the collateral inheritance tax on the balance. If he

---

1 Commonwealth v. Coleman's, Adm.   2 P. F. Smith, 472.
2 Avery's Estate.   10 Casey, 206.

neglects to do this he is chargeable with interest upon all the tax, at the rate of twelve per cent. per annum.[2]

The collateral inheritance tax, is a lien upon the real estate, chargeable with it until such tax is paid.

The estate of a decedent, composed of United States securities, passing collaterally, is subject to the payment of collateral inheritance tax.[1]

Upon payment of the collateral inheritance tax, the Administrator should take from the Register, two receipts, one to be retained by himself, the other forwarded to the Auditor-General of the State, who will countersign it as follows, and return it to the Administrator:

> AUDITOR GENERAL'S OFFICE,
> HARRISBURG, Sept. 3, 1869,

Charged, sealed, and countersigned, agreebly to the Act of May 6, 1844.

J. F. HARTRANFT,

[SEAL]

Auditor-General.

This receipt, so countersigned by the Auditor-General, is a proper voucher in the settlement of the estate, and is entitled to a credit to the amount so receipted for.

[1] Strode v. Commonwealth.   2 P. F. Smith, 189.

CHAPTER XI

INTERNAL REVENUE TAX.

By the internal Revenue Laws, it is made the duty of every Administrator to give notice to the Assessor of the District, within thirty days after he has taken charge of the estate.

This requirement is, however, seldom complied with; the usual practice being, to make the return to the Assessor, as soon as the respective shares due each distributee, can be ascertained.

The Internal Revenue Tax, payable upon Personal and Real Estate, may be seen from the following table:

	PERSONAL ESTATE.	REAL ESTATE.
Where the person taking is the wife both the real and personal estate are exempt from tax.	exempt.	exempt.
Where the person taking is the husband, the personal estate is exempt, the real estate subject to a tax of six per cent.	exempt.	6 per ct.
Where the person taking is a son, grandson, father, or grandfather, both the real and personal estate are subject to a tax of one per cent.	1 per ct.	1 per ct.

Where the person taking is a brother, or sister, the personal estate is subject to a tax of one per cent.; real estate, to a tax of two per cent.   1 per ct.   2 per ct.

Where the person taking is a nephew or niece, great nephew or great niece, both real and personal estate are subject to a tax of two per cent.   2 per ct.   2 per ct.

Where the person taking is an uncle, aunt, or cousin, both the real and personal estate are subject to a tax of four per cent.   4 per ct.   4 per ct.

Where the person taking is a brother, or sister, of the grand-parents, or descendant of the same, both the real and personal estate are subject to a tax of five per cent.   5 per ct.   5 per ct.

Where the person taking is of any other degree of relationship, or a stranger, both the real and personal estate are subject to a tax of six per cent.   6 per ct.   6 per ct.

Estates consisting of personal property, not exceeding One thousand Dollars in actual value, are not subject to tax.

Any legacy or share of personal property passing to minor children, to the extent of One thousand Dollars, is exempt from tax, where the decedent died after July 13th, 1866.

The tax is *payable*, when the party interested shall be entitled to the possession of the legacy or distributive share, and is a lien on the property for twenty years.

The Administrator should never deduct the tax in gross, from the whole balance for distribution, but the tax due on each share, should be deducted from that particular share upon which it is charged.

Under no circumstances should an Administrator or Executor pay over a distributive share or legacy, without first having paid the tax due thereon.

Where an estate is distributed, without the intervention of an auditor, the Executor or Administrator must see to the proper apportionment and adjustment of the tax due.

Where there is an auditor to report distribution, it is his duty to apportion, and report, the government tax due on each share of the estate.

CHAPTER XII.

DISCHARGE OF AN ADMINISTRATOR.

An Administrator may, by leave of the Orphans' Court having jurisdiction, make a settlement of his accounts, and be discharged from the duties of his appointment.

This can only be done, however, after his accounts have been confirmed, and the remainder of the estate in his hands surrendered to such persons as the court may direct.

Petition of Administrator to be Discharged.

To the Honorable, the Judges of the Orphans' Court of Chester County, Pennsylvania:

The petition of Samuel C. Lewis, administrator, &c., of Alexander J. Wright, late of Pennsbury township, in said county, deceased:

Respectfully represents:

That he has made a settlement of his accounts, so far as he has administered the estate committed to him, which was by this court confirmed, on the Sixteenth day of June, A. D., 1868.

That by said account, it appears that the balance of the estate remaining in his hands, amounts to Fifteen hundred ($1500) Dollars.

The petitioner, therefore prays the court to discharge him from the duties of his appointment, as Administrator aforesaid, upon his surrendering the said balance in his hands to such person as the court shall direct.

And he will, &c., &c.,

SAMUEL C. LEWIS,

Administrator, &c.

STATE OF PENNSYLVANIA, } ss.
  CHESTER COUNTY,

Samuel C. Lewis, administrator above named, being duly affirmed according to law, declares and says that the facts set forth in the foregoing petition are just and true as he verily believes.

Affirmed and Subscribed before me, this 15th day of March, 1870.
  WM. WHITEHEAD, J. P.

SAMUEL C. LEWIS.

Where property belonging to the estate comes into the hands of the Administrator after he has filed his final account, he should file a supplementary account thereof; and if he neglects or refuses, may be compelled to do so by citation.[1]

An Administrator, if he should receive rents of the real estate, does so only as agent or trustee for those to whom such real estate descends. He is not chargeable with such rents in his administration account, nor are they assets on his hands with which to pay debts.[2]

A promise by an Administrator to be personally liable for the payment of a debt of the decedent, is not binding unless in writing.[3]

Where an Administrator deposits the funds belonging to an estate in bank, he should open his account as "administrator," and the deposits should be entered to the credit of the estate, otherwise, he may be liable, in case of the insolvency of the bank where such account is kept.[4]

---

1 Shaffer's Appeal.   10. Wright, 131.
2 Harper's Appeal.   5. Wright, 50.
3 Sidle v. Anderson.   9. Wright, 468.
4 Commonwealth v. McAlister.   4. Casey, 486.

CHAPTER XIII.

THE APPOINTMENT OF GUARDIAN.

The practice prevailing in Pennsylvania, with respect to the appointment of Guardians, is, to permit the minor, when over fourteen, to appear in court, and make choice for himself.

Where the minor is under fourteen, it is customary to appoint a Guardian upon the petition of some one, usually a relative, acting as next friend.

Form of Petition where a Minor is under Fourteen.

To the Honorable, the Judges of the Orphans' Court of Chester County, Pennsylvania:

The petition of Sallie B. Davis, by her aunt and next friend, Lydia Thompson,

    Respectfully represents:

      That the petitioner is a minor child of Hamilton Davis, late of East Bradford township, County and State aforesaid, deceased, under the age of fourteen years.

That she resides in the said County, and has no one to take care of her person and estate, and prays the Court to appoint a Guardian for that purpose.

    And she will, &c.,

      SALLIE B. DAVIS,
      By her Aunt,
May 19, 1859.   LYDIA THOMPSON.

Form of Petition where a Minor is over Fourteen.

To the Honorable, the Judges of the Orphans' Court of Chester County, Pennsylvania:

The petition of Robert J. Davis,

Respectfully represents:

That the petitioner is a minor child of Hamilton Davis, late of East Bradford township, County and State aforesaid, deceased, above the age of fourteen years.

That he resides in said County, and has no one to take care of his person and estate, and prays the Court to admit him to make choice of a Guardian for the purpose aforesaid.

And he will, &c., &c.,

May 19, 1859.   ROBERT J. DAVIS.

Upon his appointment, the Guardian files in the office of the Clerk of the Courts his bond, in double the amount of the minor's estate, with two sureties, approved by the Court.

Form of Bond of Guardian.

KNOW ALL MEN BY THESE PRESENTS, That we, James T. Mullin, Josiah Philips and Amos K. Lawrence, all of the County of Chester and State of Pennsylvania, are held and firmly bound unto the Commonwealth of Pennsylvania in the sum of Four thousand Dollars lawful money of the United States of America, to be paid to the said Commonwealth, to which payment well and truly to be made, we bind ourselves, our heirs, executors, and administrators, and every of them, jointly and severally, firmly by these presents. Sealed with our seals and dated the second day of June, A. D., 1859.

WHEREAS, at an Orphans' Court held and kept at West Chester, for the said county on the fifteenth day of May, A. D., 1859. Upon the petition of Robert J. Davis, a minor child of Hamilton Davis, late of East Bradford township, deceased, said minor being over the age of fourteen years, the said James T. Mullin was appointed guardian of the person and estate of the said minor, the said James T. Mullin first entering into security in the sum of Four thousand Dollars with Josiah Phillips and Amos K. Lawrence, who were approved by the Court as sureties.

THE CONDITION OF THIS OBLIGATION IS SUCH, That if the above bounden James T. Mullin, guardian of the said Robert J. Davis, a minor child of Hamilton Davis, late of East Bradford township, deceased, shall at least once in every three years, and at any other time when required by the Orphans' Court for the County of Chester, render a just and true account of the management of the property and estate of the said minor under his care, and shall also deliver up the said property agreeably to the said order and decree of the said Court, or the directions of the law, and shall, in all respects, faithfully perform the duties of guardian of the said Robert J. Davis, then the above obligation shall be void, otherwise it shall be and remain in full force and virtue.

Sealed and Delivered in the presence of
ISAAC PARSONS.
RICHARD D. WELLS.

JAMES T. MULLIN, [L. S.]
JOSIAH PHILLIPS, [L. S.]
AMOS K. LAWRENCE. [L. S.]

This having been done, a certificate is issued by the clerk, setting forth the appointment.

Form of Certificate.

STATE OF PENNSYLVANIA, CHESTER COUNTY, } ss.

[SEAL]

I do hereby certify, that at an Orphans' Court, held at West Chester, in and for the County of Chester, the fifteenth day of May, in the year of our Lord one thousand eight hundred and fifty-nine, before the Honorable William Butler, President, and his Associates, Judges of the said Court:

THE PETITION OF Thomas J. Davis, a minor child of Hamilton Davis, late of East Bradford township, County and

State aforesaid, was presented and read, setting forth that the said minor was over the age of fourteen years, resident of said County and State, and had no person legally authorized to take charge of his person and estate: Therefore praying the said Court to appoint some suitable person as guardian for that purpose.

WHEREUPON, the said Court did, after mature deliberation, appoint James T. Mullin guardian of the person and estate of said minor, first entering into security in the sum of Four thousand dollars, with Josiah Phillips and Amos K. Lawrence, who were approved by the Court as sureties. Now therefore you, the said James T. Mullin, are hereby required and enjoined, within thirty days after any property of your ward shall have come into your hands or possession, or into the hands or possession of any person for you, to file in the office of the Clerk of the Orphan's Court, a just and true inventory and statement, on oath or affirmation, of all such property, according to the directions of the Acts of Assembly, in such case made and provided, and also to render at least once in every three years, and whenever required by the Court, a just and true account to the Orphans' Court of the County aforesaid, of the management of the property and estate of the said minor under your care, and also to deliver up the said property agreeably to the decree or order of the said Court, or the directions of law, and in all respects faithfully to perform the duties of guardian.

IN TESTIMONY WHEREOF, I have hereunto set my hand and affixed the seal of the said Court, this fifteenth day of May, in the year of our Lord one thousand eight hundred and fifty-nine.

JAMES E. McFARLAN,
Clerk.

Whenever any property of the ward comes into his possession, the Guardian must, within thirty days thereafter, file an inventory and statement, in the office of Clerk of the Courts on oath or affirmation, of all such property.

Form of Guardian's Inventory.

Inventory of James T. Mullin, guardian of the person and estate of Robert J. Davis, minor child of Hamilton Davis, late of East Bradford township, Chester County, Pennsylvania, deceased:

Cash received from Thomas S. Bell, administrator of Hamilton Davis deceased	$ 1,500	00
Judgment bond of Levi Allison, dated April 1, 1858, payable in one year with interest at six per cent	500	00
	$2,000	00

State of Pennsylvania, } ss.
    Chester County,

James T. Mullin, guardian of Robert J. Davis, minor child of Hamilton Davis, deceased, being duly affirmed, says that the foregoing is a just and true inventory and statement of all the property and estate of the said minor which has come into his hands or possession, or into the hands and possession of any person for him.

Affirmed and Subscribed before me, this 25th day of July, 1859.
    Wm. Whitehead, J. P.
                      James T. Mullin.

It is the duty of the Guardian to invest the funds of the ward, as soon as it is practicable for him to do so; and if there is any neglect in doing this, he will be chargeable with interest. Ordinarily six months should be allowed for this purpose.

Where first class real estate security cannot be found, the Guardian should petition to the Orphans' Court for authority to invest the funds of his ward in the Loan of the United

States, or of the Commonwealth of Pennsylvania, upon such terms as the Court may direct.

Form of Petition to invest Funds of Minor.

To the Honorable, the Judges of the Orphans' Court of Chester County, Pennsylvania :

The petition of James T. Mullin, guardian of Thomas J. Davis, minor child of Hamilton Davis, late of East Bradford township, Chester County, Pennsylvania, deceased,

Respectfully represents :

That, as Guardian aforesaid, he has in his possession and under his control, the sum of Fifteen hundred Dollars, the estate of the said minor, which he is desirous of investing, but has been unable to find real estate security for the same.

He, therefore, prays the Court, to make an order, directing the investment of the said sum, in the Government Loan of the United States, commonly known as "The 5-20 Loan," at such prices, or on such rates, as the Court shall think fit.

And he will, &c., &c.,

JAMES T. MULLIN,
Guardian, &c.

STATE OF PENNSYLVANIA, } ss.
  CHESTER COUNTY,

James T. Mullin, guardian above named, being duly affirmed according to law, declares and says, that the facts set forth in the foregoing petition, are just and true as he verily believes.

Affirmed and Subscribed before me,
  this 10th day of August, 1869.   } JAMES T. MULLIN.
      WM. WHITEHEAD, J. P.

It is settled, in Pennsylvania, that a Guardian cannot

(unless authorized by the will or deed of trust) invest the estate of his ward, in the stock of an incorporated company, whether a bank, railroad, canal, manufacturing or mining corporation, at the risk of such minor; with trust funds no hazards are permitted.[1]

A Guardian should permit no delay in the collection of debts due his ward; should he allow a debt to remain unsecured when it might be put beyond the reach of accidents, he becomes personally liable in case of loss.[2]

A Guardian has no control of his ward's real estate, than what relates to leasing it and receiving the rents and profits; and it is his duty to lease the land. He is bound to keep the real and personal estate safely, and to account for the personal estate, and the rents and profits of the real estate. He is bound to use the same care and management, that a prudent man would excercise in his own affairs; and must act for the ward, not for himself.[3]

A Guardian is never permitted to make money out of his ward; if any be made it must be accounted for.[4]

All investments of the ward's money, should be made by the Guardian as "guardian," and not in his own name alone.[5]

1 Worrell's Appeal. 11 Harris, 48.
2 Wills' Appeal. 10 Harris, 330.
3 Hughes' Minor's Appeal. 3 P. F. Smith, 503.
4 Eberts v. Eberts. 5 P. F. Smith, 119.
5 Morris v. Wallace. 3 Barr, 323.

CHAPTER XIV.

GUARDIAN'S TRIENNIAL AND FINAL ACCOUNT.

Every Guardian, is by law required to file, at least once in every three years, an account of his management of the minor's estate. These triennial accounts are filed in the office of the clerk of the Orphans' Court, and are for the information of the Court and the inspection of all parties concerned.

Form of Triennial Account of Guardian.

Triennial account of James T. Mullin, guardian of the person and estate of Robert J. Davis, minor child of Hamilton Davis, late of East Bradford township, Chester county, Pennsylvania, deceased.

1859.	The Guardian charges himself as follows, viz:		
25 July.	To amount of inventory filed,	2,000	00
1860.	To one year's int. on $1,500,	90	00
29 July.	To amount of legacy rec'd		
8 Sept.	from Robert L. Davis, executor of Martha Davis,		
1861.	deceased, ...	2,100	00
1 April.	To eighteen months' interest on $500, ...	45	00
29 July.	To one year's int. on $1,500,	90	00
	Amount carried forward,	$4,325	00

	Amount brought forward,	4,325	00
1 Sept.	To nine months' int. on $2,100,	94	50
1862.	To one year's int. on $500,	30	00
1 April.	To one year's int. on $1,500,	90	00
26 July.	To one year's int. on $2,100,	126	00
5 Sept.	To share of rent of real estate, for three years	900	00
		$5,565	50

1859.	The Guardian claims credit as follows:		
5 May.	By Cash paid clerk of courts for certificate of appointment,		50
25 July.	By Cash paid clerk of courts filing inventory,		50
1860.			
1 May.	By Cash paid Eliza Leonard, boarding minor, 12 months,	104	00
3 July.	By Cash paid Miss Susan Mason, tuition and school books,	38	00
15 Oct.	By Cash paid Mrs. Mary Davis, various bills of clothing for minor,	73	00
1861.			
3 June.	By Cash paid Rev. J. G. Ralston, for board and tuition, one year,	280	00
8 Nov.	By Cash paid Mrs. Mary Davis, clothing purchased for ward,	120	00
17 Nov.	By Cash paid Dr. A. K. Barnes, medical attendance,	35	00
1862.			
1 April.	By Cash paid Mrs. Eliza Leonard, board of ward,	60	00
1 June.	By Cash paid Rev. J. G. Ralston, board and tuition,	253	00
3 Aug.	By Cash paid ward traveling expenses,	50	00
	Amount carried forward,	$1,014	00

1862. 15 Oct.			
	Amount brought forward,	1,014	00
	By Cash paid Mrs. Mary Davis, clothing bills,	150	00
	By Cash paid Alexander Evans, counsel fees,	20	00
	By Cash paid clerk filing this account,		50
	Compensation to guardian,	150	00
	Balance due the estate,	4,231	00
		$5,565	50

STATE OF PENNSYLVANIA, } ss.
CHESTER COUNTY,

James T. Mullin, being duly affirmed, says, that the foregoing is a correct account of his management of his trust as Guardian of the estate of the above named Robert J. Davis, to the Fifteenth day of October, A. D., 1862.

Affirmed and Subscribed before me, this 30th day of October, 1862.
WM. WHITEHEAD, J. P.

JAMES T. MULLIN, Guardian.

A Guardian is entitled to a credit for counsel fees for professional advice necessary in the legitimate business of the trust estate, but not for collecting money lent by the Guardian at his own risk.[1]

A Guardian is not warranted in making a charge for services based upon the balance of the estate struck at the time of filing each triennial account. The law does not regard them as final accounts and to be confirmed, but only as statements from time to time of the Guardian's transactions.[2]

On the arrival of his ward at full age, the Guardian is required to settle in the Register's office (not the Clerk's) a

[1] McElhenny's Appeal. 10 Wright, 349.
[2] Foltz's Appeal. 5 P. F. Smith, 429.

full and complete account of his management of the minor's property under his care, including all the items embraced in each partial settlement; and the decree of the Orphans' Court upon such final accounts is conclusive upon all parties.

The ward should have notice in writing of the filing of such account, and in no case should a final settlement be made with the ward until the account has been passed upon and approved by the Orphans' Court. The practice of settling with wards when they have attained full age, and taking their releases without stating an account, is a bad one, and should be avoided.[1]

The final account should contain a full and complete statement of the Guardian's management of the minor's property *from the time the Guardian took charge of it.*[2]

It should embrace all the items in each triennial account, and not (as is sometimes the case) begin with the balance in the last triennial account filed.[3]

When the Guardian has the care of several minors, he must file a separate account with each of his wards.[4]

Form of Guardian's Final Account.

The final account of James T. Mullin, guardian of the person and estate of Robert J. Davis, minor child of Hamilton Davis, late of East Bradford township, Chester County, Pennsylvania, deceased—said minor having arrived at full age of twenty-one years.

---

1 Lukens's Appeal.
2 Yeager's Appeal.
3 Hughes' Minor's Appeal.
4 Baker v. Richards.

7 Watts & Sergeant, 59.
10 Casey, 177.
3 P. F. Smith, 503.
8 Sergeant & Rawle, 15.

GUARDIAN.

	The Guardian charges himself as follows, viz:		
1859.			
25 July.	To amount of inventory filed,	2000	00
1860.	To one year's int. on $1,500,	90	00
29 July.	To amount of legacy received		
8 Sept.	from Robt. L. Davis, Ex'r		
1861.	of Martha Davis, dec'd,	2100	00
1 April.	To eighteen months' int. on $500.	45	00
29 July.	To one year's int. on $1,500,	90	00
1 Sept.	To nine months' interest on		
1862.	$2,100,	94	50
1 April.	To one year's int. on $500,	30	00
26 July.	To one year's int. on $1,500,	90	00
5 Sept.	To 1 year's int. on $2,100,	126	00
1 Oct.	To share of rent of real estate,		
1863.	for three years,	900	00
3 April.	To one year's int. on $500,	30	00
25 July,	To one year's int. on $1,500,	90	00
10 Sept.	To one year's int. on $2,100,	126	00
1864.	To share of one year's rent of		
1 April.	real estate,	300	00
1 April.	To one year's int. on $500,	30	00
25 July.	To one year's int. on $1,500,	90	00
8 Sept.	To one year's int. on $2,100,	126	00
		$6,357	50
	The Guardian claims credit as follows, viz:		
1859.			
5 May.	By Cash paid clerk of courts for cert. of appointment,		50
25 July.	By Cash paid clerk, filing inventory,		50
1860.			
1 May.	By Cash paid E. Leonard, board of minor, 12 months,	104	00
3 July.	By Cash paid Susan Mason, for tuition and school books,	38	00
15 Oct.	By Cash paid Mrs. Mary Davis, various bills of clothing for minor,	73	00
	Amount carried forward,	$216	00

GUARDIAN.

1861.	Amount brought forward,	216	00
3 June.	By Cash paid Rev. J. G. Ralston, board and tuition for minor one year,	280	00
8 Nov.	By Cash paid Mrs. Mary Davis, clothing purchased for minor,	120	00
1862. 1 April.	By Cash paid Dr. A. K. Barnes, medical attendance,	35	00
1 April.	By Cash paid Mrs. Eliza Leonard for board of ward,	60	00
1 June.	By Cash paid Rev. J. G. Ralston, for board and tuition, one year,	253	00
3 Aug.	By Cash paid ward for traveling expenses,	50	00
15 Oct.	By Cash paid Mrs. Mary Davis, clothing bills,	150	00
15 Oct.	By Cash paid Alexander Evans, Esq., counsel fees,	20	00
1863. 3 May.	By Cash paid Mrs. Eliza Leonard, board of minor,	82	00
8 July.	By Cash paid Dr. J. D. White, dentist bill,	30	00
4 Sept.	By Cash paid ward for sundry expenses,	20	00
15 Sept.	By Cash paid Rev. J. G. Ralston, for tuition and board,	176	00
1864. 1 Jan.	By Cash paid Mrs. Mary Davis, for clothing purchased,	210	00
5 July.	By Cash paid to ward,	35	00
1 Sept.	By Cash paid Rev. J. G. Ralston, tuition and board,	150	00
	By Cash paid Register filing this account,	13	00
	Compensation to Guardian,	300	00
	Balance due estate,	4,157	50
		$6,357	50

State of Pennsylvania, } ss.
    Chester County,

James T. Mullin, being duly affirmed according to law,

says that the foregoing is a full and complete account of his management of the estate of the above named Robert J. Davis, under his care.

Affirmed and Subscribed before me, this 15th day of September, 1864. } JAMES T. MULLIN.
   WM. WHITEHEAD, J. P.

The compensation to Guardians varies with the peculiar circumstances of the case. Where the estate is of moderate size, and the guardianship extends over ten or twelve years, one per cent. per annum is a fair compensation, and that rate has been adopted in most of the counties of Pennsylvania.

If the estate is very small, and the trust continues only for a few years, two or three per cent per annum would be sustained, if the Guardian had been to the trouble of finding investment for the minor's estate.

In every case the true measure of compensation is the amount of labor involved or risk incurred.

If the Guardian mismanages or wastes the estate of his ward, all commissions will be denied him.

CHAPTER XV.

DUTIES OF GUARDIAN.

Sometimes it is desirable, owing to the peculiar circumstances of the minor, to expend a part of the principal in the hands of the Guardian. Where the Guardian thinks such a course prudent, he will apply by petition to the Orphans' Court for leave to expend so much of the principal as is needed, stating, at length, the grounds upon which such application is based.

Petition for leave to expend principal of Minor's Estate.

To the Honorable, the Judges of the Orphans' Court of Chester County, Pennsylvania:

The petition of James T. Mullin, guardian of the person and estate of Sallie B. Davis, a minor child of Hamilton Davis, late of West Whiteland township, Chester County, Pennsylvania, deceased.

Respectfully represents:

That the said Sallie B. Davis received from the estate of her father, Hamilton Davis, deceased, the sum of Two thousand dollars, which is now in the hands and under the control of your petitioner.

That the said Sallie B. Davis has no other estate than that above mentioned, is twenty years of age, and about to enter into matrimony.

Your petitioner therefore prays the court to direct that the sum of Three hundred dollars be paid to the said minor out of her estate now in his hands and under his control, for the purpose of enabling her to make preparation for her marriage as aforesaid,

And he will, &c., &c.,

JAMES T. MULLIN.

STATE OF PENNSYLVANIA, } ss.
CHESTER COUNTY,

James T. Mullin being duly affirmed, says that the facts set forth in the foregoing petition are just and true as he verily believes.

Affirmed and Subscribed before me, this 19th day of July, 1869.
WM. WHITEHEAD, J. P.
} JAMES T. MULLIN.

It frequently happens that the Guardian upon receiving money belonging to the ward, as in the case of a legacy, is required to execute, to the person paying it, a refunding bond.

Wherever this has been done, the Guardian, should, upon final settlement with his ward, require a similar bond, before paying such money over.

Form of Refunding Bond to Guardian.

Know all men by these presents, that we, Robert J. Davis, Andrew G. Evans and Thomas Windle, all of the County of Chester and State of Pennsylvania, are held and firmly bound unto James T. Mullin, late guardian of the said Robert J. Davis, in the sum of Four thousand two hundred Dollars, lawful money of the United States, to be paid to James T. Mullin, his certain attorney, executors, administrators and assigns, to which payment well and truly to be made we do bind ourselves, our executors and administrators jointly and severally, firmly by these presents. Sealed with our seals, dated the Nineteenth day of December, A D, One thousand eight hundred and sixty-four.

WHEREAS, Martha Davis, late of the township of West Whiteland, county and state aforesaid, deceased, by her last will and testament, gave and bequeathed to the said Robert J. Davis the sum of Two thousand one hundred Dollars, which was paid by Robert L. Davis, her executor, &c., to the said James T. Mullin, as guardian of Robert J. Davis, the said James T. Mullin executing to the said Executor a refunding bond in double the amount of said sum as required by law.

AND WHEREAS, the said Robert J. Davis having arrived at full age, and this day having had and received of the said James T. Mullin the said sum of Two thousand one hundred Dollars.

NOW THE CONDITION OF THIS OBLIGATION is such, that if the said Robert J. Davis, Andrew G. Evans, and Thomas Windle, or either of them, shall and do indemnify and save harmless the said James T. Mullin, from all loss and damage which he may or shall sustain by reason of the payment of the said Two thousand one hundred Dollars to the said Robert J. Davis, then this obligation to be void, or else to be and remain in full force and virtue.

IN TESTIMONY WHEREOF, we have hereunto set our hands and seals the day and year first above written.

Signed, Sealed, and Delivered in presence of
AMOS JONES,
JOHN EDGE.

ROBERT J. DAVIS, [L. S.]
ANDREW G. EVANS, [L. S.]
THOMAS WINDLE, [L. S.]

If, for any reason, a Guardian desires to be relieved from the duties of his appointment, he must apply by petition to the Orphans' Court.

He should at the time of filing the petition, present an account of his management of the trust; and be prepared to hand over the estate under his control, to such Guardian as the court may appoint, to succeed him.

Petition of Guardian for Discharge.

To the Honorable, the Judges of the Orphans' Court of Chester County, Pennsylvania:

The petition of James T. Mullin, guardian of the person and estate of Robert J. Davis, minor child of Hamilton Davis, late of West Whiteland township, Chester county, Pennsylvania, deceased,

Respectfully represents:

That on the Fifteenth day of May, A. D., One thousand eight hundred and fifty-nine, he was appointed by this court, Guardian of the person and estate of the said Robert J. Davis, and took upon himself the burden of said trust executing it up to this time.

That, owing to his advanced age, and the increasing demands made upon him by his private business, it is impossible for him properly to discharge his duties in the management of said minor's estate.

He therefore presents herewith an account of his administration of said trust, by which it appears, that there is a balance remaining in his hands belonging to said estate, amounting to Four thousand dollars, which said account he prays the court to confirm, and to discharge him as Guardian aforesaid, upon his surrendering the residue of the estate standing upon his account, to such person as the court shall appoint to receive the same,

And he will &c., &c.,

JAMES T. MULLIN.

STATE OF PENNSYLVANIA, } ss.
COUNTY OF CHESTER,

James T. Mullin being duly affirmed according to law, says, that the facts stated in the foregoing petition are just and true, as he verily believes.

Affirmed and Subscribed before me, this 15th day of January, 1869.
WM. WHITEHEAD,
J. P.

JAMES T. MULLIN.

The petition ought to set out the grounds upon which a discharge is asked for, and be sworn or affirmed to.

Upon the minor attaining full age, and the Orphans' Court approving of the final account of the Guardian, he may safely pay over to his ward the estate in his hands. The Guardian should take from the ward a release of all demands growing out of the guardianship. The release should be acknowledged.

Form of Release to Guardian upon final settlement with the Minor.

KNOW ALL MEN BY THESE PRESENTS, That I, Robert J. Davis, of East Bradford township, Chester county, Pennsylvania, having arrived at full age, do hereby acknowledge that I this day have had and received, of my guardian James T. Mullin, the sum of Four thousand dollars, which sum is in full satisfaction and payment of my share or dividend of the estate, real and personal, of my father, Hamilton Davis, late of East Bradford township, County and State aforesaid, deceased, as well as of a legacy from the estate of my aunt, Martha Davis, late of said County, deceased; and by these presents I do hereby release, acquit, and forever discharge the said James T. Mullin, his heirs, executors and administrators, of and from the said guardianship, and of and from the said dividends, shares and legacies, as well as from all actions, suits, payments, accounts, claims and demands whatsoever, for or by reason thereof, or of the estates hereinfore mentioned.

IN WITNESS WHEREOF, I have hereunto set my hand and seal, this Nineteenth day of December, A. D., One thousand eight hundred and sixty-four.

Signed, Sealed, and Delivered in presence of
MATTHEW BAKER,
THOS. BARTHOLOMEW.

ROBERT J. DAVIS, [L. S.]

CHAPER XVI.

ASSIGNMENT FOR THE BENEFIT OF CREDITORS.

While the laws of Pennsylvania expressly forbid the preference of creditors, in the deed of assignment itself, yet an insolvent debtor may prefer any creditor by giving him a judgment bond before executing the deed of assignment.

The principle is now well settled in this State, that so long as a debtor retains dominion over his property, he may prefer one creditor to another, and that such preference is not fraudulent in law or in fact.[1]

If, therefore, one about to make an assignment, desires to protect any particular creditor in preference to the rest, he should execute a judgment bond for the amount of his indebtedness, and have it entered in the Prothonotary's office before executing a deed of assignment.

If such an one has money borrowed from his wife, he may secure her against loss by executing to some one as her trustee, a judgment bond for the amount, and entering it in the Prothonotary's office before the execution of the deed of assignment.

Or, where he holds any money *in trust* for third parties, he should see that a judgment bond is properly executed therefor, and entered in advance of the execution of his assignment.

Judgment bonds given to secure creditors in the manner just indicated, ought to be entered in the Prothonotary's office *a day in advance of the execution* of the deed of assign-

---

[1] Uhler *v.* Maulfair,
Mellon's Appeal.
York County Bank *v.* Carter.
Keen *et. al. v.* Kleckner.
11 Harris, 484.
1 Grant, 214.
2 Wright, 455.
6 Wright, 530.

ment. If this be done, it does away with the necessity of proving which was first, and leaves no doubt as to who is entitled to preference. Although in a contest between a judgment bond and a deed of assignment, where there was no proof as to which was first, the Supreme Court held that the judgment had precedence of the assignment.[1]

In a case where it was *proven* that the deed of assignment was executed on the same day in which a judgment was entered, but at an earlier hour, it was held that the assignment took precedence, and passed the real estate free from the lien of such judgment.[2]

The deed of assignment should contain a clause, reserving from the operation of the instrument, all the wife's separate estate.

The exemption of three hundred dollars by the person making the assignment, must be expressly claimed in the deed of assignment, or else it is deemed to have been waived.[3]

The three hundred dollars reserved, should be out of "the *real* or *personal* estate" of the persons assigning.

The deed of assignment should also confer power upon the assignee to sell "at either *public* or *private* sale."

The deed of assignment should have a five cent internal revenue stamp affixed to it.

Form of Deed of Assignment for the benefit of Creditors.

THIS INDENTURE, made the Twentieth day of December, A. D., One thousand eight hundred and sixty-nine, between Francis Hickman, of the township of Londonderry, Chester county, Pennsylvania, and Mary L., his wife, of the one part, and Benjamin F. Wickersham of the township of Franklin, County and State aforesaid, of the other part.

WHEREAS, the said Francis Hickman, owing to sundry losses and misfortunes, is at present unable to discharge his

---

1 Buchanan's Appeal.
2 Mechanics' Bank v. Gorman.
3 Blackburne's Appeal.

1 P. F. Smith, 438.
8 Watts & Sergeant, 308.
3 Wright, 166.

just debts and liabilities, and is willing to assign all his property for the benefit of his creditors.

Now THIS INDENTURE WITNESSETH, That the said Francis Hickman, and Mary L., his wife, as well in consideration of the premises, and for the purpose of making a just distribution of his estate and effects among the creditors of the said Francis Hickman, as also of the sum of one dollar to them in hand paid by the said Benjamin F. Wickersham, the receipt whereof is hereby acknowledged, have granted, bargained, sold, assigned, transferred, and set over, and by these presents do grant, bargain, sell, assign, transfer, and set over unto the said Benjamin F. Wickersham his heirs and assigns, all the messuages, lands, tenements, and hereditaments wherever situate, and all the goods, chattels and effects, and property of every kind, real, personal, and mixed, of the said Francis Hickman, (excepting and reserving from the operation of this assignment such an amount of property, real and personal, as is by law exempt from levy and sale on execution and distress for rent, by virtue of the Act of April 9, A. D., 1849, and saving and excepting also all the separate property of the said Mary L. Hickman, which she holds or is in any manner entitled to.)

To HAVE AND TO HOLD, receive and take the same to the said Benjamin F. Wickersham, his heirs and assigns, to the proper use and behoof of the said Benjamin F. Wickersham, his heirs and assigns forever.

IN TRUST however, and to the intent and purpose, that he the said Benjamin F. Wickersham, shall and do, as soon as convenient, sell and dispose, at public or private sale, of all the lands, tenements, goods, chattels, and property of every kind, of the said Francis Hickman, and collect and recover all the outstanding claims and debts to him the said Francis Hickman, due, and with the moneys arising therefrom, after deducting his, the said Benjamin F. Wickersham's reasonable costs and charges, shall and do pay the creditors of the said Francis Hickman their respective just demands in full, if there shall be sufficient assets to satisfy the whole, and if there shall not be sufficient assets to satisfy all the demands of the creditors in full, then equitably and ratably according to the amount of their respective demands, and according to law.

And should any part or portion of said trust property or funds remain after fully complying with the trust aforesaid, then the said Benjamin F. Wickersham shall deliver over and reconvey the same unto the said Francis Hickman, his heirs, executors, administrators and assigns, in a reasonable time thereafter.

In Testimony Whereof, the said Francis Hickman, and Mary L., his wife, have hereunto set their hands and seals the day and year first above written.

Signed, Sealed, and Delivered in the presence of
    Levi Preston,
    G. G. Downing.

Francis Hickman. [l. s.]
Mary L. Hickman. [l. s.]

5 Cent Internal Revenue STAMP.

State of Pennsylvania, } ss.
  County of Chester,

Before me, a Justice of the Peace, in and for the State and County aforesaid, personally appeared, the above named Francis Hickman, and Mary L. Hickman, his wife, and in due form acknowledged the foregoing deed of assignment to be their act and deed, and desired that the same might be recorded as such according to law. The said Mary L., being of full age, and by me duly examined, separate and apart from her said husband, and the contents thereof being first made known to her, declared that she did voluntarily, and of her own free will and accord, seal, and as her act and deed, deliver the said indenture, without any coercion or compulsion of her said husband.

In testimony whereof, I have hereunto set my hand and seal, this Twentieth day of December, A. D., 1869.

                    Wm. Whitehead, [seal.]
                           J. P.

I hereby accept the trust specified in the foregoing deed of assignment. Witness my hand, this Twenty-eighth day of December, A. D., 1869.

B. F. WICKERSHAM.

The deed of assignment should be put in the hands of the Assignee as soon after its execution as it is practicable to do so, for the thirty days allowed by law in which to record the deed, begin to run from the date of its execution.

Where the Assignee named in a deed of assignment declined to accept the trust, and another was appointed in his stead, the Supreme court held, that the thirty days allowed by law, in which to record the deed, ran from its date, and not from the time of the appointment of the new Assignee.[1]

The deed of assignment must be recorded in the office of the Recorder of Deeds, in the county in which the Assignor resides, within thirty days after the execution thereof. It may be placed upon record by the party making the assignment, or by any one having a legal or beneficial interest. If not recorded within thirty days, the deed is null and void as against any of the creditors of the party making the assignment.

The deed of assignment must be recorded not only in the county where the Assignor resides, but also in every county where his real estate is situated.[2]

---

[1] Johnson v. Herring.   10 Wright, 420.
[2] Dougherty v. Darrach.   3 Harris, 399.

CHAPTER XVII.

INVENTORY AND APPRAISEMENT.

The first step required to be taken by the Assignee upon assuming the duties of his trust, is to petition the Court of Common Pleas of the county, for the appointment of two persons to appraise the estate and effects assigned.

This petition, if the Court be not in session, may be presented to any judge during vacation. An associate judge has power to appoint such appraisers.

Form of Petition for Appraisers.

To the Honorable, the Judges of the Court of Common Pleas of Chester County, Pennsylvania:

The petition of Benjamin F. Wickersham,

    Respectfully represents:

      That on the Twentieth day of December, A. D., One thousand eight hundred and sixty-nine, Francis Hickman, of the township of Londonderry, in said county, and Mary L., his wife, executed a voluntary deed of assignment of all the property, real and personal, of the said Francis Hickman, to the petitioner in trust, for the benefit of the creditors of the said Francis Hickman.

The petitioner, therefore, prays the Court to appoint two

disinterested and competent persons to appraise the estate and effects so assigned.

And he will, &c., &c., &c.,

December 27, 1869.   B. F. WICKERSHAM.

STATE OF PENNSYLVANIA, } ss.
  COUNTY OF CHESTER,

Benjamin F. Wickersham, being duly affirmed according to law, says, that the facts set forth in the foregoing petition are just and true as he verily believes.

Affirmed and Subscribed before me,
  the 28th day of December, 1869.   } B. F. WICKERSHAM.
    WM. WHITEHEAD, J. P.

Form of Certificate of Appraisers.

STATE OF PENNSYLVANIA, } ss.
  COUNTY OF CHESTER,

[SEAL OF COURT.]   The Commonwealth of Pennsylvania, to John B. Rogers and Levi Davis, greeting:

WHEREAS, Benjamin F. Wickersham, did by his petition represent to the Court of Common Pleas for the said county, that Francis Hickman, of Londonderry township, in said county, and Mary L., his wife, on the Twentieth day of December, A. D., One thousand eight hundred and sixty-nine, did execute to the petitioner, a voluntary assignment of all the property, real and personal, of the said Francis Hickman, in trust for the benefit of the creditors of the said Francis Hickman; and praying the said Court to appoint two disinterested and competent citizens to appraise the property so assigned; and the said Court having appointed you as the appraisers of said property agreeably to the prayer of the petitioner, you are, therefore, hereby required to execute the duties of said appointment, according to the directions of the Act of Assembly in such case made and provided.

Witness the Honorable William Butler, President of our said Court, at West Chester, the Twenty-first day of December, in the year of our Lord, One Thousand eight hundred and sixty-nine.

ALFRED RUPURT,
Prothonotary.

The appraisers upon being appointed by the Court, must be sworn or affirmed to discharge their duties with fidelity.

Form of Oath of Appraisers.

STATE OF PENNSYLVANIA, } ss.
   COUNTY OF CHESTRR,

John B. Rogers and Levi Davis, appraisers appointed by the annexed order to appraise the estate and effects assigned by Francis Hickman, and Mary L., his wife, to Benjamin F. Wickersham, in trust for the creditors of the said Francis Hickman, being duly affirmed, say that they will, well and truly, and according to the best of their judgment, appraise the estate and effects so assigned.

Affirmed and subscribed before me, the 5th day of January, 1870.
   WM. WHITEHEAD, J. P.

JOHN B. ROGERS,
LEVI DAVIS.

ASSIGNEE.

Inventory and Appraisement of the estate and effects of Francis Hickman, assigned to Benjamin F. Wickersham, in trust for the benefit of creditors.

One Horse,	150	00
One Cow,	75	00
Wagon,	30	00
Harness,	15	00
Two Hogs,	30	00
Plough,	12	00
Sulky,	26	00
Manure,	10	00
75 Acres of land in Londonderry township, Chester county, Pennsylvania, at $80,	6000	00
	$6,348	00

Appraised by us, this 5th day of January, 1870.

JOHN B. ROGERS,
LEVI DAVIS.

The inventory and appraisement should include all the estate, *real* and *personal*, of the person making the assignment. The fee of the appraisers is one dollar per day for every day employed.

Immediately following the inventory, should be an affidavit by the Assignee, that the inventory includes all the property assigned to him.

Form of Affidavit by the Assignee.

STATE OF PENNSYLVANIA, } ss.
CHESTER COUNTY,

Benjamin F. Wickersham, assignee above named, being duly affirmed according to law, declares and says, that the foregoing is a full and complete inventory of the estate and effects of Francis Hickman, assigned to him in trust for creditors, so far as the same have come to his knowledge.

Affirmed and Subscribed before me, the 5th day of January, 1870. } B. F. WICKERSHAM.
    WM. WHITEHEAD, J. P.

The order from the Prothonotary appointing the appraisers, the affirmation of the appraisers, the inventory and appraisement, as well as the affidavit of the Assignee, should be upon the same sheets of paper, or, if on different ones, then all fastened together and filed in the Prothonotary's office, *within thirty days of the date of the assignment.*

During the thirty days allowed by law for the Assignee to file an inventory of the estate assigned, the goods may remain in the possession of the person making the assignment,[1] and are in the meantime not liable to execution.[2]

As soon as the Assignee has filed his inventory in the Prothonotary's office, he must give bond in double the amount of the inventory, with two securities to be approved by the Court.

This bond may be approved by one of the Judges of the Court, and during vacation. The bond must be filed in the Prothonotary's office.

Form of Assignee's Bond.

KNOW ALL MEN BY THESE PRESENTS, That we, Benjamin F. Wickersham, assignee of Francis Hickman, of Londonderry township, Chester county, Pennsylvania, and Mary L., his wife, in trust for the benefit of creditors of the said Francis Hickman, David Steele and Amos Kerns, all of Chester county, Pennsylvania, are held and firmly bound

---

1 Dallam v. Fitler.   6 Watts & Sergeant, 325.
2 Mitchell v. Willock.   2 Watts & Sergeant, 254.

unto the Commonwealth of Pennsylvania, in the sum of Twelve thousand six hundred and ninety-six ($12,696) Dollars, lawful money of the United States, to be paid to the said Commonwealth, her certain attorney or assigns, to which payment well and truly to be made we bind ourselves jointly and severally firmly by these presents. Sealed with our seals, dated the 13th day of January, in the year of our Lord, One thousand eight hundred and seventy.

The condition of this obligation is such, that if the above bounden, Benjamin F. Wickersham, assignee of Francis Hickman, as aforesaid, shall in all things comply with the provisions of the Acts of Assembly in such case made, and shall faithfully execute the trust confided to him, then the above obligation to be void, or else to remain in full force and virtue.

| Sealed and Delivered in the presence of SAMUEL STARR, ANDREW BLACK. | B. F. WICKERSHAM. [SEAL.] DAVID STEELE. [SEAL.] AMOS KERNS. [SEAL.] |

The fact of the Assignee's bond not having been approved by the Court within thirty days from the execution of the deed, will not invalidate the assignment.[1]

An Assignee may act before his bond has been approved and filed.

The title and the power vest in the Assignee from the execution of the assignment, and he does not have to wait until the inventory is filed and bond approved.[2]

Whenever the person executing the deed of assignment, has reserved to himself $300 in accordance with the Exemption law of 9 April, 1849, the Assignee should have an inventory and appraisement made of the property thus set apart, to the amount of Three hundred Dollars.

This appraisement should be made by the appraisers of the rest of the assigned estate.[3] If the exemption has not

---

1 Heckman et. al. v. Messinger. 13 Wright, 473.
2 Dallam v. Fitler. 6 Watts & Sergeant, 326.
3 Mulford & Shirk. 2 Casey, 475.

been *expressly claimed* by the person making the assignment *in the deed itself*, the Assignee has no right to set apart such property to the Assignor, and should the Assignee do so, he may properly be charged with the amount so set apart.[2]

Form of Inventory and Appraisement of $300 exempted in Deed of Assignment.

STATE OF PENNSYLVANIA, } ss.
    CHESTER COUNTY,

John B. Rogers and Levi Davis, appraisers of the estate and effects of Francis Hickman, of Londonderry township, County and State aforesaid, assigned to Benjamin F. Wickersham in trust for the benefit of creditors, being duly affirmed say that they will well and truly appraise and set apart property of said Francis Hickman to the value of Three hundred Dollars, as reserved by him in the deed of assignment, in accordance with the Act of Assembly of April 9, 1849.

Affirmed and Subscribed before me, }   JOHN B. ROGERS.
  the 5th day of January, 1870.   LEVI DAVIS.
    WM. WHITEHEAD, J. P.

There are no special directions in the law as to how this appraisement should be made and where filed; the better practice, however, seems to be, to have the inventory and appraisement made by the appraisers of the whole estate, and file the paper in the Prothonotary's office, along with the general inventory.

The Three hundred Dollars worth of property taken by the Assignor, must not, of course, be included in the general inventory, as the Assignee is in no way chargeable with the same.

[2] Blackburne's Appeal.   [3] Wright, 166.

Inventory and Appraisement of property elected to be retained by the above named Francis Hickman, under the reservation contained in the deed of assignment to Benjamin F. Wickersham, in trust for benefit of creditors.

Bureau,		12
Bedsteads,		16
Doz. Chairs,		18
Stove,		10
Table,		13
Bedding,		18
Carpet,		24
Looking Glass,		5
Wash-Stand,		4
Book-Case,		12
Wagon,		50
Harness,		15
Hay,		20
Plough,		13
Horse,		70
		$300 00

Appraised by us, the 5th of January, 1870.

JOHN B. ROGERS,
LEVI DAVIS.

If, from any cause, the exemption of Three hundred dollars has not been expressly claimed in the deed of assignment, the person assigning, may, by a late act of assembly, apply to the Court of Common Pleas, of the county, to have set aside for the use of himself and family, articles of household furniture or things of domestic use, not exceeding in value, Three hundred dollars.[1]

This application cannot be made until after the appraisement, and the Court may, if no cause be shown to the contrary, after notice to creditors, order that the same be released from the assigned estate and handed to the Assignor.

[1] Act of 4 May, 1864. Pamphlet Laws, 762.

Form of Petition of Assignor to have Property set aside for use of himself and family.

To the Honorable, the Judges of the Court of Common Pleas of Chester county, Pennsylvania.

The Petition of Francis Hickman, of Londonderry township, County and State aforesaid:

Respectfully represents:

That by virtue of a deed of assignment, executed on the Twentieth day of December, One thousand eight hundred and seventy-nine; all his estate, real, personal and mixed, was assigned to Benjamin F. Wickersham, of said County, in trust, for the benefit of his creditors.

That all of the property, so assigned, has been duly appraised and an inventory of the same filed of record.

The petitioner prays the Court, to have set aside, for the use of himself and family, out of the property so transferred, articles of household furniture, not exceeding in value, at the appraisement thereof, Three hundred dollars; according to the provisions of the Act of May 4, A. D., 1864, "relating to assignments in trust for creditors,"

And he will, &c., &c.,

January 18th, 1870. FRANCIS HICKMAN.

STATE OF PENNSYLVANIA, } ss.
COUNTY OF CHESTER,

Francis Hickman, above named, being duly affirmed according to law, declares and says, that the facts stated in the foregoing petition are just and true, as he verily believes.

Affirmed and Subscribed before me,
this 15th day of January, 1869. FRANCIS HICKMAN.
WM. WHITEHEAD,
J. P.

CHAPTER XVIII.

DUTIES OF ASSIGNEES.

The inventory and appraisement having been filed, and the bond given and approved, the Assignee should give public notice, in a newspaper published in the County, once a week, for six successive weeks.

Form of Notice to Debtors and Creditors.

ASSIGNEE'S NOTICE.

Notice is hereby given, that Francis Hickman, of Londonderry township, Chester county, Pennsylvania, and Mary L., his wife, by deed of voluntary assignment, have assigned all the estate, real and personal, of the said Francis Hickman, to Benjamin F. Wickersham, of Franklin township, in said County, in trust, for the benefit of the creditors of the said Francis Hickman. All persons, therefore, indebted to the said Francis Hickman, will make payment to the said Assignee, and those, having claims or demands, will make known the same, without delay.

B. F. WICKERSHAM,
Assignee of Francis Hickman.

December 30, 1869.

It is the duty of the Assignee, to at once take prompt and active measures, to collect all the debts due the person assigning. Wherever claims cannot be collected without legal proceedings, the Assignee should institute them at once. By such a course, it can be ascertained whether the personal estate will reach an amount sufficient to pay the debts not secured by lien. If, in the judgment of the Assignee, it becomes necessary to sell the personal property, at public sale; he should advertise and sell, observing the same directions as were given (on page 20 and 21) to Administrators in disposing of the personal property of a decedent.

The Assignee must bear in mind, that he takes the land of the person assigning, subject to all the liens entered against it, up to the time of the assignment; that he cannot sell the land, and make a clear title for it, without first having these lien creditors to release and allow him to do so.

It is, almost always, to the interest of lien creditors to release to the Assignee, and permit him to sell rather than have the Sheriff do so under execution, as land will usually command a better price when sold in this way than at a forced sale. *All* of the lien creditors must join such release.

Form of Agreement of Lien Creditors to Release Real Estate and allow Assignee to sell.

THIS AGREEMENT, made the Second day of April, A. D., One thousand eight hundred and seventy, between Benjamin F. Wickersham, assignee of Francis Hickman, and Mary L., his wife, in trust, for the benefit of the creditors of the said Francis Hickman, of the one part, and James Thomas, Henry Brown and Levi Jackson, judgment and lien creditors of the said Francis Hickman, of the other part.

WHEREAS, the real estate of the said Francis Hickman, is insufficient to pay and discharge all the liens, by judgment and otherwise, against it:

AND WHEREAS, in our opinion, it will be to the advantage of all persons interested, that the said real estate should be sold by the said Assignee, rather than by the Sheriff of the County:

AND WHEREAS, at our request, the said Assignee has agreed to proceed and make sale of the same, upon our agreeing to release our respective liens against the said real estate.

Now this agreement witnesseth, that for and in consideration of the premises, and of the said Assignee agreeing to proceed and make sale of the said real estate, we, the said James Thomas, Henry Brown and Levi Jackson, do hereby covenant, promise and agree, to, and with, the said Benjamin F. Wickersham, assignee as aforesaid, that we, and each of us, shall and will, upon the said Benjamin F. Wickersham, assignee as aforesaid, making a contract of sale of the said real estate, forthwith or soon as required, after such contract of sale, enter or cause to be entered, full and complete release of and discharge of said real estate of and from said liens, whether by judgment or otherwise, so as to enable the said Assignee to make a conveyance, clear of incumbrances, to the purchaser of the real estate.

It is further agreed, that the money arising from said sale, after defraying the costs and expenses incident to the said sale and assignment, shall be paid to the respective lien creditors of the said Francis Hickman, in the order of their respective liens, so far as the proceeds of the said sale, after deducting said expenses, shall extend to pay the same, each lien having preference according to its seniority, according to law.

In witness whereof, we have hereunto set our hands and seals, the day and year first above mentioned.

Signed, Sealed, and Delivered in the presence of
John Wood,
James Todd,

B. F. Wickersham, [seal.]
James Thomas, [seal.]
Henry Brown, [seal.]
Levi Jackson, [seal.]

A creditor who has his claim secured by a judgment or mortgage on the real estate assigned, is nevertheless entitled to a dividend *on his whole claim* out of the proceeds of the personal property.[1]

1 Shunk's Appeal. 2 Barr, 309

And where the real estate assigned has been sold, and the claim of the lien creditor partly paid by the proceeds of such sale, he is still entitled to a *pro rata* dividend *on his whole claim* out of the personal property, and is not limited to a dividend upon his claim as reduced.[1]

And the same is true where personal property used as collateral security was sold, and the proceeds appropriated to part payment of the debt; the creditors being entitled to a dividend upon the whole amount of their claim at the date of the assignment.[2]

In all assignments for the benefit of creditors, wages of miners, mechanics and laborers, are preferred debts; and to the extent of One hundred dollars entitled to be paid before any creditors of the Assignor.

Where, however, there are a large number of such claims, and any question arises as to their right to be preferred, it would not be prudent for an Assignee to pay workmen in advance of other creditors. The safer course is for the Assignee to file his account and allow distribution to be made by an auditor.

Claims for labor are not entitled in a distribution of the proceeds of land, to preference over lien creditors.[3]

1 Morris v. Olwine.   10 Harris, 443.
  Miller's Appeal.   11 Casey, 483.
2 Patten's Appeal.   9 Wright, 160.
3 Wade's Appeal.   5 Casey, 328.
  Johnston's Estate.   9 Casey, 516.

CHAPTER XIX.

ACCOUNT OF ASSIGNEE &C., &C.

An Assignee for the benefit of creditors, should file an account of his administration of the trust, within one year from the date of the assignment,

This account is filed in the office of the Prothonotary of the Court of Common Pleas, and the fee for filing and advertising the same should be included, by the Assignee, in his account.

The account of an Assignee must, in every instance, be under oath or affirmation.

The law has fixed no rule with regard to the compensation of Assignees. The same fees as are allowed to Executors and Administrators, have been recognized as proper for Assignees. It has long been settled in Pennsylvania, that trustees are entitled to reasonable compensation for their services, though there be no stipulation on the subject in the deed of assignment.

"The amount of compensation," says Judge Woodward, "must depend on the discretion, which is nothing else than the reason and conscience of the tribunals having jurisdiction of the trust. In the admeasurement of it, regard is to be had to the amount and character of the estate, and to the labor, skill, and success, attending the administration of it."[1]

As we have said before, in speaking of the compensation of administrators, five per cent. upon sales of personal property, and three per cent. upon sales of real estate, are the customary fees allowed.

[1] Heckert's Appeal. 12 Harris, 486.

Form of an Assignee's Account.

The Account of Benjamin F. Wickersham, assignee of Francis Hickman, of Londonderry township, Chester county, Pennsylvania, and Mary L. his wife, in trust for the benefit of the creditors of the said Francis Hickman.

The accountant charges himself as follows, viz:—		
To amount of inventory filed in Prothonotary's office,	6,348	00
To Cash received from the Chester County Insurance Co.,	12	00
To advance on real estate above appraisement,	200	00
	$6,560	00

The accountant claims credit as follows, viz:—		
By Cash paid for recording deed of assignment,	2	10
By Cash paid appraisers,	2	00
By Cash paid Henry T. Evans for advertising and printing,	3	68
By Cash paid Levi Doan, tax,	8	59
By Cash paid William Whitehead, Esq., Justice fees,	1	00
By Cash paid Prothonotary,	3	60
By Cash paid Prothonotary for filing this account,	6	00
By Cash paid John Scott, Esq., counsel fee,	100	00
By compensation to accountant	175	00
Balance due the estate,	6,258	03
	$6,560	00

Errors Excepted }
July 14, 1870, }

B. F. WICKERSHAM,
Assignee, &c.

STATE OF PENNSYLVANIA, } ss.
COUNTY OF CHESTER,

Benjamin F. Wickersham, assignee above named, being duly affirmed according to law, declares and says, that the foregoing is a just and true account of the administration of the property and estate assigned and transferred to him by Francis Hickman, in trust for the benefit of creditors.

Affirmed and Subscribed
before me, the 14th day
of July, 1870.   B. F. WICKERSHAM.
Wm. Whitehead,
J. P.

An Assignee in making out his account, should charge himself in the first instance with the whole amount of the inventory of the property assigned.

He is then entitled to credit for all money paid out either in the payment of debts or necessary expenses.

He is also entitled to credit for all debts that could not be collected by due diligence, and for losses on sales of personal property, if it has been fairly sold.[1]

It rarely happens that an Assignee can safely venture to distribute the balance of the assigned estate in his hands, without the aid of an auditor. Such a course is not to be advised, as questions are likely to arise which he cannot solve, while the confirmation of his account by the Court, and the distribution of the balance by an Auditor, relieves the Assignee, and puts the responsibility elsewhere.

Petition for Auditor to distribute balance in hands of Assignee.

To the Honorable, the Judges of the Court of Common Pleas of Chester County, Pennsylvania:

The petition of James Pierce, respectfully represents:

That Benjamin F. Wickersham, Assignee, &c., of Francis Hickman, of said

[1] Patton's Estate.   2 Parsons, 104.

county, has filed an account of his administration of said trust, which was confirmed *nisi* by this Court on the Fifth day of August, A. D., One thousand eight hundred and seventy.

That there is a balance of said estate in the hands of the Assignee, amounting to Six thousand two hundred and fifty-eight dollars and three cents, and that your petitioner is a creditor of the said Francis Hickman, and interested in the distribution thereof.

He therefore prays the Court to appoint an auditor, to make distribution of said balance amongst the parties entitled thereto.

And he will &c., &c.,
JAMES PIERCE.

The petition should be under oath or affirmation.

When the report of the Auditor has been made and confirmed by the Court, a duly certified copy of the distribution, as reported by him, should be obtained from the Prothonotary, and to it attached a receipt to be signed by all of the distributees.

Form of Receipt to Assignee.

Received, November 15, 1870, of Benjamin F. Wickersham, Assignee of Francis Hickman, of Londonderry township, Chester county, Pennsylvania, and Mary L., his wife, in trust, for the benefit of the creditors of the said Francis Hickman, the respective amounts sets opposite our names in the accompanying schedule, in accordance with the report of Alexander Evans, Esq., Auditor appointed by the Court of Common Pleas, of Chester county, to report distribution of said estate in the hands of the said Assignee.

Then should follow the names, and opposite to them, the amount paid each.

CHAPTER XX.

Internal Revenue Stamps.

No stamp is necessary upon an instrument executed prior to October 1, 1862, to make it admissible in evidence or to entitle it to record.

Either party to an instrument may affix the stamp *before* execution.

When two or more persons join in the execution of an instrument, the stamp to which the instrument is liable under the law may be affixed and cancelled by either of them.

The Supreme Court of Pennsylvania, have decided, that it is the duty of the party *selling* real estate, to put the stamp upon the deed and of course to buy and pay for it, if the person buying has not expressly agreed to do it for him.[1]

Of course, the buyer and seller can make their own agreement, about who shall pay for the stamps, and, where they do so, that agreement is law as to them. But where the only agreement is that the purchaser is to "receive a deed properly executed" by the seller, the seller must purchase the stamps and affix them to the deed.

Letters of Administration.

Where the estate does not exceed One thousand
  dollars in value, no stamp is required.   no stamp.
Where it exceeds One thousand dollars, and does
  not exceed Two thousand dollars in value, a
  one dollar stamp is required. $1.00
Every additional One thousand dollars, or fractional part thereof over Two thousand dollars
  in value, a fifty cent stamp.   50

[1] Callaghan v. McCredy, *et. al.*   12 Wright, 465.

Administrator's Bond.

Where value of the estate is under One thousand dollars, no stamp is required. — no stamp.

Where the value of the estate exceeds One thousand dollars, a one dollar stamp. — $1.00

Guardian's Bond.

The same as Administrator's.

Receipt.

For any sum over Twenty dollars, a two cent stamp. — 2

For delivery of any property, no stamp is required. — no stamp.

Promissory Note.

For any sum not exceeding One hundred dollars, a five cent stamp. — 5

For every additional One hundred dollars, or fractional part thereof over One hundred dollars, a five cent stamp. — 5

Deed.

Where consideration does not exceed Five hundred dollars, a fifty cent stamp. — 50

Where consideration exceeds Five hundred dollars, but does not exceed One thousand dollars, a one dollar stamp. — 1.00

For every additional Five hundred dollars, or fractional part thereof over One thousand dollars, a fifty cent stamp. — 50

Bond or Mortgage.

For any sum exceeding One hundred dollars, and not exceeding Five hundred dollars, a fifty cent stamp. — 50

Exceeding Five hundred dollars, and not exceeding One thousand dollars, a one dollar stamp. — 1.00

For every additional Five hundred dollars, or fractional part thereof over One thousand dollars, a fifty cent stamp. — 50

BANK CHECK.
A two cent stamp. 2
AGREEMENTS.
A five cent stamp. 5

A mere *copy* of an instrument is not subject to stamp duty unless it is a certified one, in which case a five-cent stamp should be affixed to the certificate of the person attesting it; but when an instrument is executed and issued in duplicate, triplicate, &c., as in the case of a lease of two or more parts, each part has the same legal effect as the other, and each should be stamped as original.

Upon any assignment of a mortgage, a stamp is required equal to that conferred on the original instrument.

Indorsements of payments of interest on bonds, mortgages, etc., require no stamp, although in the form of a receipt.

Upon every assignment, or transfer of a mortgage upon which payments have been made, the same stamp is required as would be required by an original mortgage given *for the amount still remaining unpaid.*

The stamp duty upon letters of administration, must be appropriate to the value of the estate to be administered upon. If the administrator has no control over the real estate (as he generally has not, except for the payment of debts) the stamp is regulated by the value of the personal estate.

The stamp duty on letters of administration, covers all subsequent papers in the settlement of the estate.

A contract for the sale of land, or to make a title-deed to the purchaser on the payment of the purchase money, requires a five-cent stamp as an agreement for each sheet or piece of paper upon which it is written.

INDEX.

A.

ADMINISTRATION,
    who is entitled to, 9.
    right to, of widow and children, 9.
    renunciation of, 9.

ADMINISTRATOR,
    to give security, 10.
    has no control over real estate, 11.
    to give notice to debtors and creditors, 11.
    to file inventory, 13.
    to take receipts, 14.
    to appraise widow's $300, 16.
    to file widow's inventory, 18.
    should sign conditions of sale, 20.
    may permit property to be taken at appraisement, 22.
    must petition for order of sale of real estate, 23.
    to give bond before selling real estate, 26.
    to give thirty days notice of sale, 27.
    must describe real estate fully, 28.
    may adjourn sale of real estate, 32.
    to make return to order of sale, 32, 33.
    to prepare deed for real estate sold, 34.
    to pay preferred debts in their order, 38
    to petition for auditor to make distribution, 39.
    to require surrender of bond on its payment, 40.
    should take directions to satisfy, 40.
    should take fee for recording mortgage, 41.
    to file an account within a year, 42.
    compensation of, 43, 44.
    to give notice to distributees, 45.
    to invest funds after a year, 45.

ADMINISTRATOR. *Continued.*

    to require refunding bonds, 45.
    should take releases, 46.
    to give bond for collateral tax, 49.
    to file collateral inventory, 53.
    may appeal from collateral appraisement of personal estate, 53.
    must not pay collateral tax on real estate out of personal estate, 53.
    to pay collateral tax on balance not in dispute, 53.
    to take duplicate receipts for collateral tax, 54.
    to give notice to Internal Revenue Assessor, 55.
    must deduct legacy tax from each share, 56.
    must pay tax before paying share over, 57.
    discharge of, 58.
        form of petition for, 58.
    must file supplementary account, 59.
    is not chargeable with rents in his account, 59.
    promise of, to pay debt of decedent, 59.
    should deposit in bank as "administrator," 59.

ADMINISTRATOR'S ACCOUNT,

    form of, 42. 43.
    must be filed within a year, 42.
    should include fee for filing, 42.
    supplementary, in certain cases, 59.
    rent not chargeable in, 59.

ADVERTISEMENT,

    form of, 28. 29.
    how made, 28. 94.

ADJOURNMENT,

    of sale of real estate, 32.

AGREEMENT,

    stamp on, 103.
    with purchaser of real estate, 31.
    with sureties of purchaser of real estate, 31. 32.
    of assignee, with lien creditors, 94. 95.

APPRAISERS, (*See Collateral Appraiser.*)

    fees of, in decedent's estates, 14.
    appointment of, in assigned estates, 84. 85.
    fees of, in assigned estates, 87.

AUDITOR,

    petition for, in decedent's estates, 39.
    should apportion legacy tax, 57.
    petition for, in assigned estates, 99. 100.

ASSIGNEE,

to petition for appraisers, 84.
affidavit of, as to amount of assigned estate, 87.
to give bond, 88.
may act before giving bond, 89.
title vests in, from execution of assignment, 89.
to have exempted property appraised, 89.
duties of, 94.
notice of, to creditors, 93.
must collect debts due assignor, 93.
may sell personal property, 94.
agreement of, with lien creditors, 94. 95
to file an account within one year, 97.
compensation of, 97.
petition of, for an auditor, 99. 100.
should take receipt after auditor reports distribution, 100.

ASSIGNEE'S ACCOUNT,

form of, 98.
should be filed in Prothonotary's office, 97.
should be under oath or affirmation, 97.
manner of stating, 99.

ASSIGNMENT,

for benefit of creditors, 79.
  preference of creditors in, 79.
  exemption must be claimed in, 80.
  deed of, 80. 81. 82.
  stamp on, 82.
  deed of, must be recorded in county where assignor resides, 83.
  deed of, must be recorded within thirty days, 83.
  may be recorded by any one having interest, 83.
  if not recorded within 30 days, void as to creditors, 83.
  must be recorded wherever assignor owns real estate, 83.
of bond, stamp on, 103.

B

BOND,

of administrator, 10. 11.
  stamps on, 11. 102.
  for sale of real estate, 27.
  for collateral tax, 49.
of guardian, 61.
  stamps on, 102.
refunding to guardian, 75. 76.

BOND. (Continued.)

 of assignee, 88. 89.
  must be approved by court, 88.
  must be filed in Prothonotary's office, 88.
 as to payment of, 40. 41.
 direction to satisfy, 40.
 fee for satisfaction of, 41.
 stamps on, 102.

C.

COMPENSATION,

 of appraisers, 14.
 of administrators, 43. 44.
 of collateral appraisers, 53.
 of guardians, 73.
 of appraisers in assigned estates, 87.
 of assignees, 97.

COLLATERAL TAX,

 upon what estates payable, 49.
 payable on estate passing to grandmother, 49.
 estate devised to wife or widow's son not liable, 49.
 estate less than $250 not subject to, 49.
 bond for, 49. 50.
 on real estate must not be paid out of personalty, 53.
 is five per cent, 53.
 discount for prompt payment of, 53.
 tax if not paid within a year, 53.
 is lien on real estate, 54.
 due on estate composed of U. S. Securities, 54.
 duplicate receipts for, to be taken, 54.

COLLATERAL APPRAISER,

 appointment of, 50.
 must be sworn or affirmed, 51.
 affidavit of, 51.
 fees of, 53.

COLLATERAL INVENTORY,

 form of, 52.
 must include real estate, 52.
 should be filed in Register's office, 53.

CONDITIONS OF SALE,

 of personal property, 20. 21.
 of real estate, 29. 30.

CONDITIONS OF SALE. *Continued.*
must be signed by administrator, 29.
should be read by auctioneer, 29.
stamps on, 31, 103.

CREDITORS,
notice to, 12. 93.
release from, to allow assignee to sell, 94. 95.
rights of, in assigned estates, 95. 96.
petition of, for auditor in decedent's estate, 39.
petition of, for auditor in assigned estate, 99. 100.

D.

DISTRIBUTION,
of decedent's estate, 45.

DEED,
for real estate sold by order of Court, 34. 35. 36.
stamp on, 36. 102.
of assignment for benefit of creditors, 80. 81. 82.
stamp on, 102.

E.

EXEMPTION,
in deed of assignment, 80.
must be claimed or assignee cannot set apart, 90.
inventory and appraisement of, 90. 91.
petition for, when not claimed in deed, 92.

F.

FUNERAL EXPENSES,
payment of, 38. 39.

FEES,
for entering satisfaction, 41.
for recording, should be collected, 41.

GUARDIAN,
appointment of, 60.
where minor is under fourteen, 60.
where minor is over fourteen, 61.

GUARDIAN. *Continued.*

to file bond, 61.
certificate of, 62.
to file inventory within thirty days, 63
form of inventory of, 64.
must invest funds of minor, 64.
should petition for leave to invest, 65.
investments by, 66.
should lease real estate of minor, 66.
petition of, for leave to invest, 65.
duties of, 66.
triennial account of, 67. 68. 69.
is entitled to counsel fees, 69.
form of final account of, 70. 71. 72. 73.
duties of, 70.
compensation of, 73.
may expend principal by leave of court, 74.
petition of, for leave to expend principal, 74. 75.
may require refunding bond, 75.
form of refunding bond to, 75. 76,
petition of, for discharge, 77.
release to, 78.

GUARDIAN'S ACCOUNT,

triennial must be filed, 67.
    form of, 67. 68. 69.
    filed in Clerk's office, 67.
must be filed when minor comes of age, 70.
final, 70. 71. 72.
    is filed in Register's office, 69.

II.

HEIRS,

must pay collateral tax on real estate, 53.

I.

INTERNAL REVENUE STAMPS,

may be affixed by either party *before* execution, 101.
may be affixed by either party where two join, 101.
on deed, by whom affixed, 101.
    to be affixed by person selling, 101.
on letters of administration, 101. 103.
on administrator's bond, 102.

INDEX.

INTERNAL REVENUE STAMPS. *Continued.*
 on guardian's bond, 102.
 on receipt, 102.
 on promissory note, 102.
 on deed, 102.
 on bond, 102.
 on mortgage, 102.
 on bank check, 103.
 on agreement, 103.
 not required upon copy of an instrument, 103.
 on assignment of bond and mortgage, 103.
 on contract for sale of land, 103.

INTERNAL REVENUE TAX,
 amount of, payable on real and personal estate, 55. 56.
 not payable on personal estates less than $1000, 56.
 not payable on certain legacies to minors, 56.
 is *payable*, when party is entitled to possession, 56.
 is lien for twenty years, 56.
 should be paid before legacy is paid over, 57.

INVENTORY,
 general must be filed within thirty days, 13.
  form of, 14.
  should include personal, not real estate, 14.
  is filed in Register's office, 13.
 of guardian, 64.
  is filed in Clerk's office, 63.
 of assignee, 87.
  must be filed within thirty days, 88.
  must be filed in Prothonotary's office, 88.
 of widow's election, 17.
  must be filed in Clerk's office, 18.
 of $300 retained in assigned estates, 91.
  should be filed in Prothonotary's office, 90.

J.

JUDGMENT,
 direction to satisfy, 40.

L.

LIEN CREDITOR,
 release of, to assignee, 94. 95.
 entitled to dividend on whole estate, 95. 96.

LETTERS OF ADMINISTRATION,
 to whom granted, 9.
 stamps on, 101. 103.

M.

MEDICINE,
 furnished decedent, a preferred debt, 38.

MORTGAGE,
 payment of, 40. 41.
 satisfaction of, 41.
 fee for entering satisfaction of, 41.
 stamps on, 102.
  assignment of, 103.

MARRIED WOMAN,
 may execute release without her husband, 48

MINOR,
 petition of for guardian, 60. 61.

N.

NOTICE,
 to debtors and creditors, 11. 93.
  form of, 12. 93.
 of sale of personal property, 20. 94.
 of sale of real estate, 27. 28.
 must be given by administrator to distributees, 45.

O.

ORDER OF SALE,
 petition for, 23.
 return to, 32. 33.

P.

PERSONAL PROPERTY,
 sale of, 20.
 conditions of sale of, 20. 21.

PERSONAL PROPERTY. *Continued.*

vendue list of, must be filed, 21.
may be taken at appraisement, 22.
certificate of Register as to amount of, 24.
may remain in possession of assignor, 88.
collateral inheritance tax on, 53.

PETITION,

for sale of real estate, 23. 24.
for auditor to distribute, 39. 40.
of administrator for discharge, 58. 59.
for guardian, 60. 61.
for leave to invest minor's estate, 65.
for leave to expend principal of minor's estate, 74. 75.
of guardian for discharge, 77.
for appraiser of assigned estate, 84. 85.
to have property set aside for assignor, 92.
for auditor to distribute in assigned estates, 99. 100.

PROMISSORY NOTE,

given for property sold, 21.
surety in, sign along with maker, 21.
stamp on, 102.

PURCHASER,

of real estate, agreement with, 31.
sureties of, 32.

PURCHASE MONEY,

terms of payment of, 32.

R.

REAL ESTATE,

descends to heirs and not to administrator, 11.
administrator cannot rent, 11.
petition for sale of, 23. 24.
statement of, 25.
sale of, must be public, 27.
should be well described in advertisement, 28.
advertisement of, 28. 29.
conditions of sale of, 29. 30.
adjournment of sale of, 32.
return to sale of, 32. 33.
deed for, 34. 35. 36.
collateral tax upon, 53.
duties of guardian in respect to, 66.
agreement for sale of, by assignee, 94. 95.

RECEIPT,
should specify on what account given, 15.
form of, to administrator, 15.
from widow for $300, 16.
for personal property taken at appraisement, 22.
for collateral inheritance tax, 54.
to assignee after auditor's report, 100.

REFUNDING BOND,
should be required by administrator, 45.
    form of, 45. 46.
to guardian in certain cases, 75.
    form of, 75. 76.

RELEASE,
to administrator, 47.
married woman may execute, 48.
to guardian on final settlement with minor, 78.
of lien creditors, to allow assignee to sell, 94, 95.

RENUNCIATION,
of right to administration, 9.
    must be signed by all having a right, 9.
    filed in Register's office, 9.

RENT,
payment of, 38.
should not be charged in administrator's account, 59.
not assets with which to pay debts, 59.
to be collected by guardian, 66.

RETURN,
to order of sale for payment of debts, 32. 33.

S.

SURETY,
should sign along with the maker of a note, 21.
of administrators, ought to own real estate, 26.

SALE,
of real estate must be public, 27.
    twenty days notice should be given, 27.
    conditions of, 29. 30. 31.
    may be adjourned, 32.
    must be reported to the Court, 32.
of personal property, 20. 21. 94.
    conditions of, 20. 21.

T.

TAX, (*See Collateral Tax.*)
(*See Internal Revenue Tax.*)

V.

VENDUE LIST,
    must be filed within thirty days of sale, 21.

W.

WAGES,
    not exceeding a year, a preferred debt, 38.
    not confined to *last* year of decedent's life, 39.
    in assigned estates, 96.
        not entitled to preference over lien creditors, 96.

WIDOW,
    renunciation of, 9.
    may elect to retain $300, 16.
    receipt of, for $300 in money, 16.
    acceptance by, of articles appraised, 18.
    right of, to retain $300 in certain cases, 19.

WIDOW'S INVENTORY,
    form of, 16. 17.
    to be filed by administrator, 18.
    to be made by appraisers of other property, 16.
    must be approved by Court, 18.
    to be filed in Clerk's office, 18.

www.ingramcontent.com/pod-product-compliance
Lightning Source LLC
Chambersburg PA
CBHW030404170426
43202CB00010B/1488